OECD Competition Trends 2024

OECD
BETTER POLICIES FOR BETTER LIVES

Please cite this publication as:
OECD (2024), *OECD Competition Trends 2024*, OECD Publishing, Paris, https://doi.org/10.1787/e69018f9-en.

ISBN 978-92-64-46637-1 (print)
ISBN 978-92-64-84598-5 (pdf)
ISBN 978-92-64-34369-6 (HTML)
ISBN 978-92-64-83301-2 (epub)

OECD Competition Trends
ISSN 3005-4494 (online)

Photo credits: Cover illustration by Ferdio based on © phochi/Gettyimages.

Corrigenda to OECD publications may be found on line at: www.oecd.org/about/publishing/corrigenda.htm.

Foreword

This fifth edition of OECD Competition Trends presents unique insights into global competition trends based on data from 77 OECD and non-OECD jurisdictions. It analyses multi-year data on a large number of economic and legal indicators in the OECD CompStats database with a focus on the main developments in 2022. In doing so, OECD Competition Trends 2024 supports informed policy making and contributes to improving competition law and policy around the world.

The OECD Competition Committee, which includes representatives of the world's major competition authorities, is the premier source of policy analysis and advice to governments on how best to harness market forces in the interests of greater global economic efficiency and prosperity. For over 60 years, the OECD and its Competition Committee have taken a leading role in shaping the framework for international co-operation among competition agencies. The resulting recommendations, best practices and policy roundtables serve both as models and inspiration for national initiatives and as tools for sharing global best practices on competition law and policy. Competition officials from developed and emerging economies are offered a unique platform from which to monitor developments in competition policy and enforcement, and to discuss new solutions for increasing effectiveness.

The OECD CompStats database is the result of an initiative launched in 2018. The database compiles general statistics relating to competition agencies, including data on enforcement and resources and information on advocacy initiatives. The data are collected annually and currently covers the period 2015-22. The data are mainly presented at an aggregate level, combining the data of individual jurisdictions. The aggregate-level analyses focus on (i) all participating jurisdictions ("All jurisdictions"), (ii) two groups consisting of OECD and non-OECD jurisdictions, and (iii) four geographic regions (Americas, Asia-Pacific, Europe and Middle East and Africa (MEA)). This year, participating jurisdictions have agreed to make public their data pertaining to merger control. Therefore, the data in that section is not only presented on an aggregated basis. The objective is not to rank jurisdictions, which is not possible given the specificities of their merger regimes, however it does allow to better understand the data and address jurisdiction-specific phenomena.

In this year's report, some numbers from earlier years may differ from previous versions of the OECD Competition Trends series for several reasons, including: (i) Costa Rica has been included this year in OECD averages as it became an OECD Member on May 2021, making 2022 its first full year as a Member; (ii) some jurisdictions provided information that was not available in previous years; and (iii) some jurisdictions provided revised statistics for some variables.

As the role and scope of competition law and policy continue to evolve, the tools of competition authorities must constantly develop and incorporate lessons learned from others. This publication contributes to helping policy makers and competition enforcers to stay up to date with the different ways in which competition law and policy is applied throughout the world.

The publication was prepared by the OECD Competition Division, in particular a team composed of Wouter Meester, project leader; Daniel Westrik; Aura García Pabón; Manuela Sánchez and Alberto Gómez, all of the OECD Competition Division. The report benefited from comments and suggestions by Ori Schwartz and Antonio Capobianco, respectively Head and Deputy Head of the OECD Competition Division. The report was prepared for publication by Erica Agostinho. The authors thank the individual competition authorities in the participating jurisdictions who provided the information on which much of this publication is based.

Table of contents

FIGURES

INFOGRAPHICS

TABLES

Executive summary

This report focuses on the main developments in global competition enforcement in 2022. The OECD CompStats database currently includes eight years of data from 77 jurisdictions. An Excel file with a complete set of graphs covering all competition enforcement indicators, i.e. all indicators on all years (2015-22), can be found on the OECD Competition Trends publication website.

The report consists of three chapters. Chapter 1 provides a brief overview of competition enforcement in the participating jurisdictions. Chapter 2 describes the main developments in 2022 compared to 2021, for resources, cartel and abuse of dominance enforcement, and advocacy. Chapter 3 presents a more detailed (in-focus) analysis of merger control data and trends, including a review of all merger prohibitions between 2015-22.

Key developments in 2022

This section covers the key developments in 2022 for resources, cartel enforcement, abuse of dominance enforcement, and advocacy. Merger control is covered in a subsequent standalone chapter.

Resources

Competition staff continued growing – There was continued growth in the number of competition staff in 2022, although the growth was lower than in 2021. The average number of competition staff per competition authority was 130 in 2022, up from 125 in 2021, and considerably higher than 118 in 2020. There was an increase in every region except Asia-Pacific. The average number of competition staff increased in every year from 2015 to 2022.

Nominal competition budget increased but real budget decreased – Average nominal competition budget increased in all regions except Asia-Pacific. The highest increase (18.1% compared to 2021) was seen by non-OECD jurisdictions, mostly driven by two of them. However, average real competition budget decreased in all regions. This suggests that the significant increase in annual growth rate for nominal competition budget (10%) in 2022 across all jurisdictions, was predominantly due to inflation, as it was negative at -2.6% for real competition budget.

Cartel enforcement

Leniency applications increased in all regions for the first time since 2015 – For the first time since 2015, when the OECD began collecting the Competition Statistics data, the total number of leniency applications increased in all regions, reversing the previous downward trend. The total number of leniency applications increased from 201 in 2021 to 248 in 2022, an annual growth rate of 23.4%. The resurgence began in 2021 in Europe, continuing in 2022, and accompanied by an increase in all regions.

Cartel ex-officio investigations increased by 19.3% – Average cartel ex-officio cartel investigations increased to 8.4 in 2022 (representing an annual growth of 19.3%), countering the steady decline from 14.7 in 2016 to 7.1 in 2021.

Cartel dawn raids remained stable – The average number of cartel dawn raids remained stable in 2022 (with an average across all jurisdictions of 3.6 in 2022, identical to 2021), slightly increasing in the Americas and Europe, while decreasing in Asia-Pacific and MEA. In all regions, we had witnessed a significant decline in 2020, mostly resulting from the Covid-19 lockdowns.

Cartel decisions decreased, mostly in Europe – In 2022, there was a decline in the average number of cartel decisions in Europe and MEA but an increase in Americas and Asia-Pacific. The average across all jurisdictions fell from 6.8 in 2021 to 6.3 in 2022. The biggest decline was in Non-OECD European jurisdictions, where the annual decrease on cartel decisions was around 41%. Two possible explanations for the decline in cartel decisions include the decrease in ex-officio investigations between 2016 and 2021 (including decrease in investigations due to covid during 2020-21) and the consistent decline in leniency applications since 2015.

Cartel bid-rigging decisions increased by 9.7% – There was an increase in bid-rigging cases between 2021 and 2022 (the only two years for which OECD CompStats data for bid-rigging decisions exist), namely from 154 to 169. The average number of bid-rigging decisions across all jurisdictions increased by 9.7% in 2022. As a percentage of all cartel decisions, bid-rigging decisions across all jurisdictions increased from 32% in 2021 to 38% in 2022, although there were some regional differences. In 2022, the region where bid-rigging decisions represented the highest percentage of cartel decisions was MEA (40%).

The industries with the most cartel decisions in 2022 were manufacturing, construction and wholesale trade – The top 10 industries based on the total number of cartel decisions remained relatively similar to the ranking in 2021. "Manufacturing", "Construction" and "Wholesale Trade" were still the three industries with the most cartel decisions in 2022. However, they only represented 44% of all cartel decisions in 2022, down from 48% in 2021. "Agriculture, forestry, fishing and hunting" was the industry where the number of cases grew the most, representing 7% of the cases in 2022 (up from only 2.4% in 2021).

Cartel settlements decreased, notably in MEA – The average number of cartel cases with settlements was relatively stable in 2022, albeit with regional differences. Notably, in MEA, the average cartel cases closed with settlements decreased from 4.3 to 2.9.

Abuse of dominance enforcement

Abuse of dominance investigations declined in 50 jurisdictions – The average number of abuse of dominance investigations launched by competition authorities declined in all regions, except MEA. In 82% (50 out of the 63 jurisdictions with relevant data for all years), the number of investigations declined or remained unchanged. The average number of investigations launched was down from 5.6 in 2021 to 4.2 in 2022 across all jurisdictions, a decline of around 25%.

Abuse of dominance decisions kept their downward trend – The average number of abuse of dominance decisions per jurisdiction declined slightly overall, from 2 in 2021 to 1.5 in 2022. This continues a slow downward trend over the period, from an average of 2.4 abuse of dominance decisions per jurisdiction in 2015 to 1.5 in 2022. Despite the increase observed in 2021, there was a significant decrease in the number of abuse of dominance decisions in both OECD and non-OECD jurisdictions, reverting to 2020 levels.

The industries whith the most abuse of dominance decisions in 2020 were manufacturing, transportation and wharehousing, and information – The top 10 industries based on the total number of abuse of dominance decisions in 2022 was similar to 2021. "Manufacturing", "Transportation and

Warehousing" and "Information" remained in the top three industries with the highest number of abuse of dominance decisions in 2022, representing 47% of total decisions.

Abuse of dominance settlements and commitments declined notably in Americas – The average number of abuse of dominance cases in which settlements, plea bargain procedures, commitment procedures, or other types of negotiated/consensual procedures for settling infringement cases were used slightly declined in 2022, however this was mostly driven by the Americas, while in other regions such as Europe and MEA, their use increased.

Sanctions

Fines imposed by competition authorities decreased in 2022 – Fines for both cartels and abuse of dominance cases declined in 2022. The average abuse of dominance fine imposed per jurisdiction declined 52% from 42.5 million euros in 2021 to 20.4 million euros in 2022. The average cartel fine imposed per jurisdiction decreased 45% from 89.8 million euros in 2021 to 49.5 million euros in 2022.

Advocacy

Market studies increased in Asia-Pacific – The average number of market studies per jurisdiction was relatively stable in all regions, except Asia-Pacific where it increased considerably (from 3.2 in 2021 to 5.4 in 2022).

In focus: trends in merger control

Each edition of OECD Competition Trends includes a chapter that addresses a certain topic in more detail. This year's edition focuses on merger control.

Merger notifications dropped in 2022 – In 2022, there was a drop in the number of overall merger notifications predominantly driven by a decline in OECD jurisdictions. The number of merger notifications in non-OECD jurisdictions continued to increase in 2022, although at a slower rate than in 2021.

Merger intervention rate increased significantly in OECD jurisdictions – Contrary to 2021, there was a significant increase in the merger intervention rate – the proportion of transactions in which competition authorities intervened, either by imposing a remedy or by prohibiting a transaction – in 2022. Most of this increase was driven by OECD jurisdictions, while there was a slight decline for non-OECD jurisdictions.

Competition authorities approved more mergers with remedies – The rising overall intervention rate in 2022 has been mostly driven by an increase in the use of remedies (which increased by more than 55%), rather than prohibitions and withdrawn mergers which remained relatively stable.

Prohibitions are concentrated in a few jurisdictions –The five jurisdictions with the most prohibitions represent 54% of all prohibitions during the period 2015 to 2022 (116 of 216 prohibitions). This includes South Africa, United States, United Kingdom, Israel and the European Union.

Horizontal theories of harm are the most common in prohibition decisions – Horizontal theories of harm make up the vast majority in merger prohibition decisions. Most are horizontal unilateral theories of harm, while horizontal coordinated theories of harm are similar in amount to vertical theories of harm. Conglomerate and public interest theories of harm are negligible in merger prohibition decisions.

The industries with most prohibitions between 2015-22 were manufacturing, retail trade, and transportation and warehousing – Prohibitions are more common in industries that are typically characterised by homogenous products and where there may be more likely issues related to a horizontal overlap, such as manufacturing, retail trade and transportation and warehousing.

Infographic 1. Key facts and figures

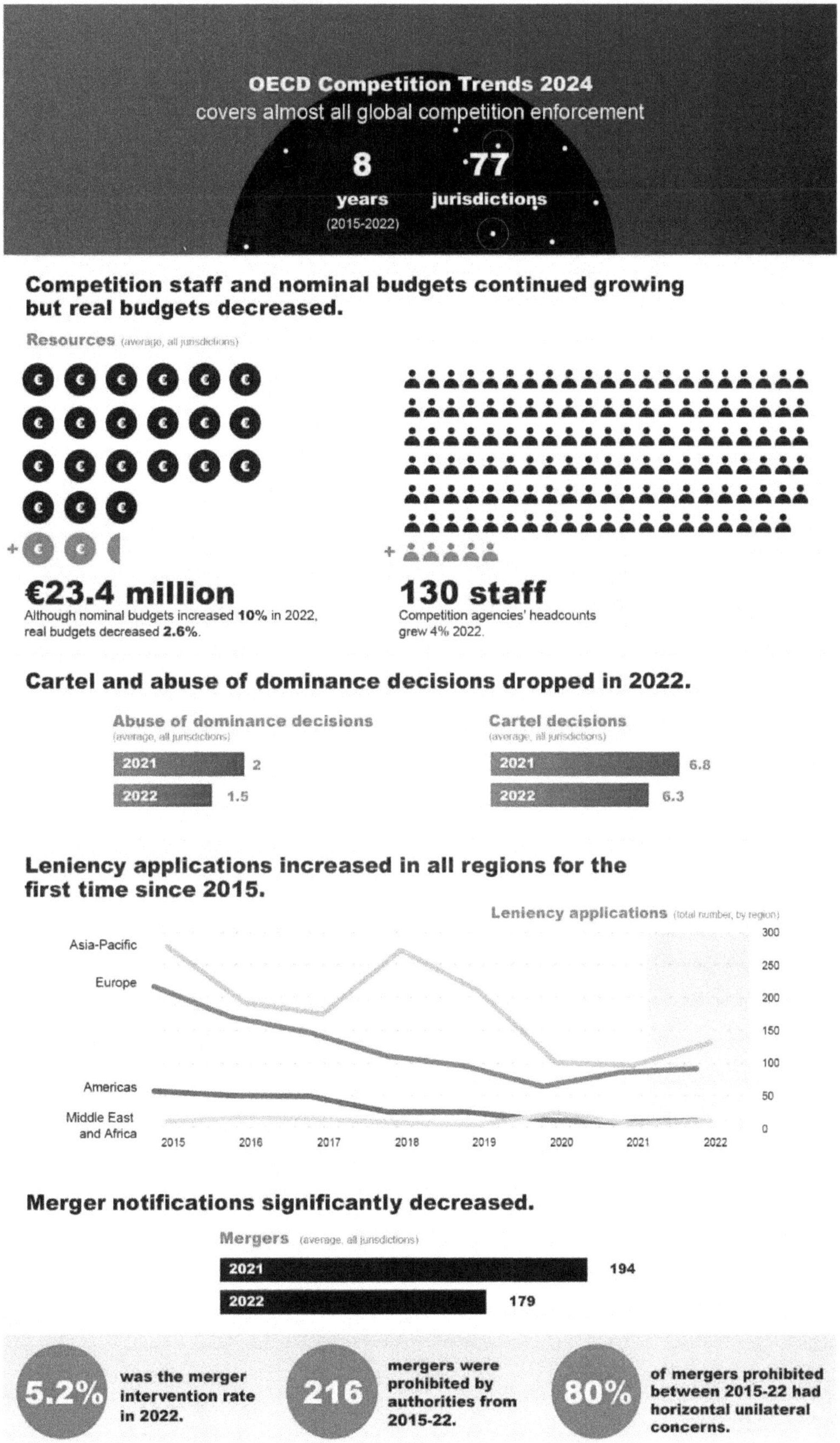

1 OECD CompStats at a glance

This chapter describes the coverage of the report and presents a snapshot of the competition resources and enforcement activity of the CompStats jurisdictions.

Regional coverage of the OECD CompStats database

In this report, the OECD CompStats database includes 77 jurisdictions. The following figure presents the number of participating jurisdictions by region. The complete list of jurisdictions in each region is included in the Annex, together with the lists of the competition authorities that provided data in each jurisdiction.

Figure 1.1. Regional coverage of the OECD CompStats Database 2023

Source: OECD CompStats database.

StatLink https://stat.link/5gxrsz

Available data in the CompStats database

The OECD CompStats database temporal coverage increased from seven to eight years due to the additional year of data for 2022. The OECD CompStats website contains the underlying data for each of the CompStats variables in this report.

Snapshot of competition resources and enforcement activity

The general overview below provides a snapshot of competition resources and enforcement activity.

Figure 1.2. Competition resources and enforcement activity, 2022

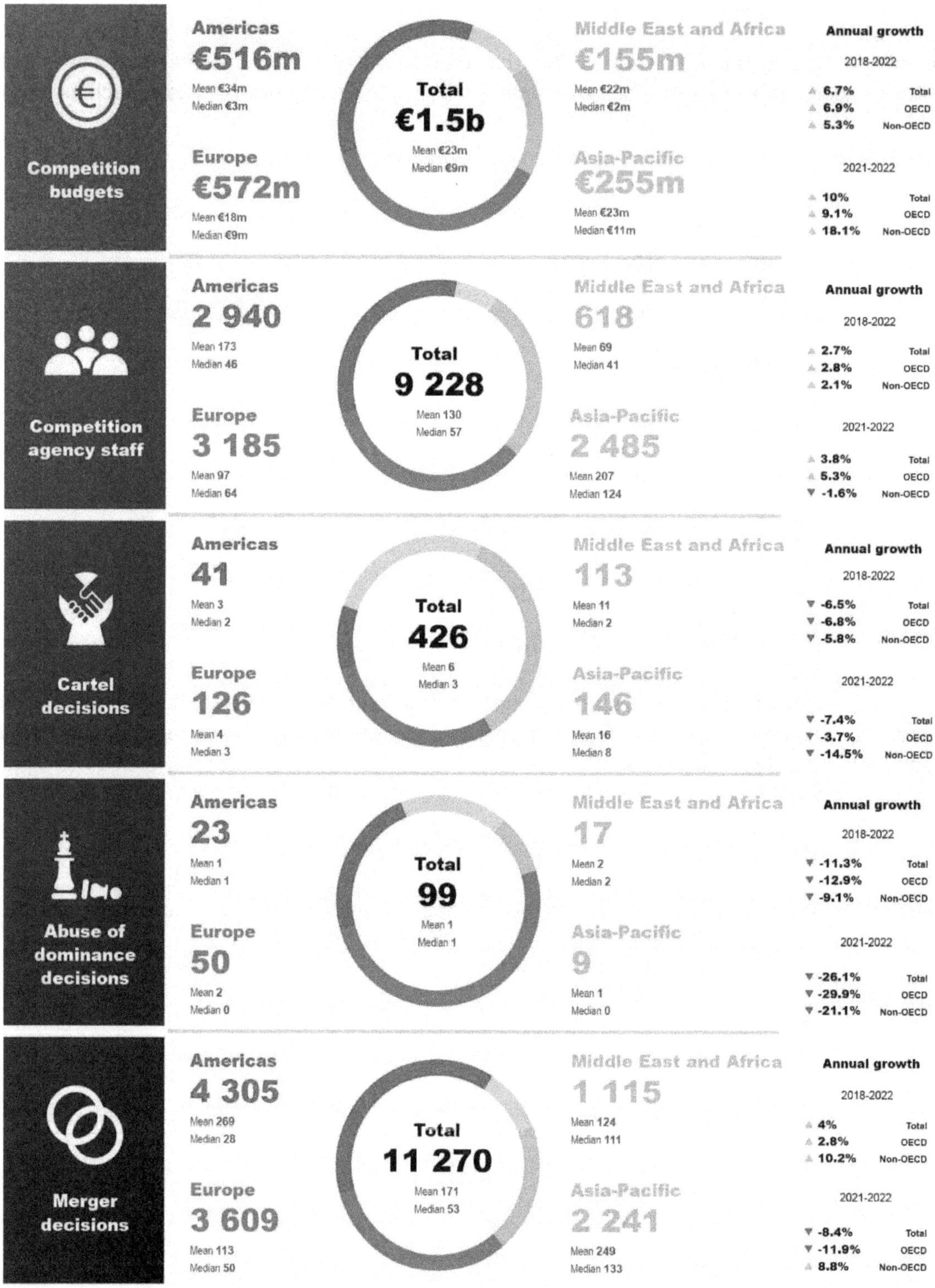

Note: All measures based on the number of jurisdictions that provided all eight years of data (64 jurisdictions for nominal competition budget, 71 jurisdictions for competition staff, 68 jurisdictions for cartel decisions, 68 jurisdictions for abuse of dominance decisions, and 66 jurisdictions for merger decisions). Nominal competition budget figures are in 2015 euros (non-euro currencies are converted using 2015 official exchange rates on 31 December 2015) to eliminate distortions due to currency fluctuations. The growth on nominal budget for non-OECD jurisdictions was mostly driven by two of them. Competition staff are staff working only on competition (excluding administrative staff or staff involved in other functions of the authority, such as consumer protection, public procurement, sector regulation).
Source: OECD CompStats database.

2 Key developments in 2022

This chapter highlights the main global competition enforcement developments in 2022. It contextualises them among the broader trend over time, where relevant. It includes the most significant changes in variables such as resources, cartel enforcement, abuse of dominance enforcement, and advocacy. Merger control has a dedicated chapter that follows this one, and thus does not feature here.

As for last year's OECD Competition Trends report, this edition focuses on the main annual developments, that is, the key changes in 2022 relative to 2021.

Resources

Competition staff continued to grow

The sustained growth in competition staff at authorities around the world continued in 2022, with an overall annual growth rate of 3.8% (although this was around half the annual growth rate of 6% in 2021). The average number of competition staff per agency increased from 125 in 2021 to 130 in 2022, considerably higher than the average of 118 in 2020. There was an increase in every region except Asia-Pacific. The average number of competition staff increased in every year from 2015 to 2022, except in 2020 where it remained the same as in the previous year. The regional differences in staff levels are largely driven by differences in the size of the jurisdictions.

Figure 2.1. Average number of competition staff per competition authority all (left) and by region (right), 2015-22

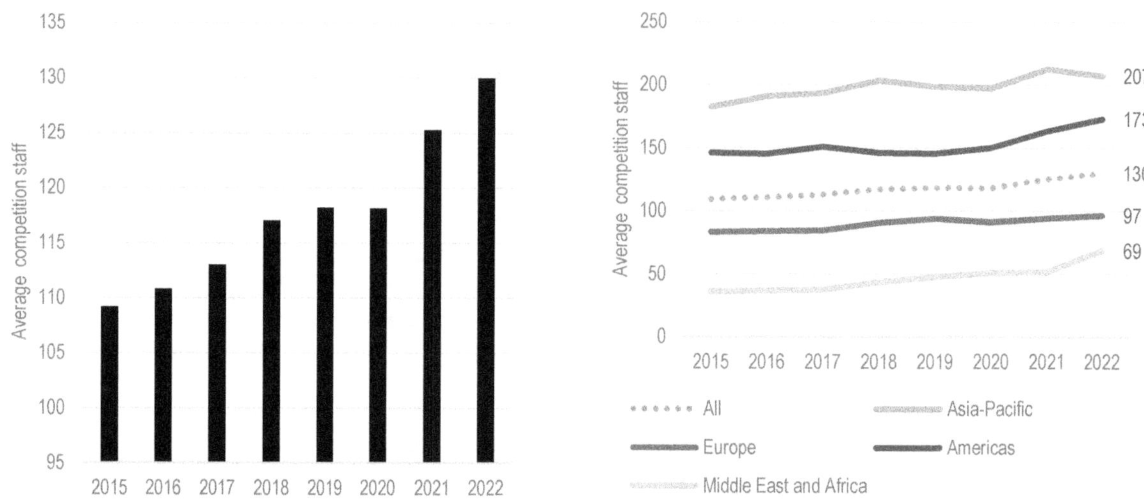

Note: Data based on the 71 jurisdictions in the OECD CompStats database that provided data for competition staff for eight years.
Source: OECD CompStats database.

StatLink https://stat.link/3vuzrb

Nominal competition budget increased, but real competition budget was flat

The average nominal competition budget increased in 2022 in all regions, except Asia-Pacific. Thus, there was a decline in both competition staff and budget in Asia-Pacific in 2022.

However, average real competition budget decreased in all regions.[1] The significant increase in annual growth rate for nominal competition budget (10% in 2022 across all jurisdictions) appears to be predominantly driven by inflation, as the real growth was negative at -2.6%.

Particularly stark was the large increase in nominal budget in MEA jurisdictions in 2022 (52.7%), although in real terms the average competition budget for the region decreased by 1.5%. While inflation was an issue across the region, there was one single MEA jurisdiction that had particularly high inflation in 2022 and explained most of the large difference between nominal and real competition budget. A similar trend can be observed in the Americas region. While the growth in the nominal competition budgets in the region was of 11.5%, mostly driven by two jurisdictions, the average real competition budget decreased in 1.1%. As it is the case with staff, the regional differences in budget levels are largely driven by differences in the size of the jurisdictions.

Figure 2.2. Average nominal (left) and real (right) competition budget (euros), by region, 2015-22

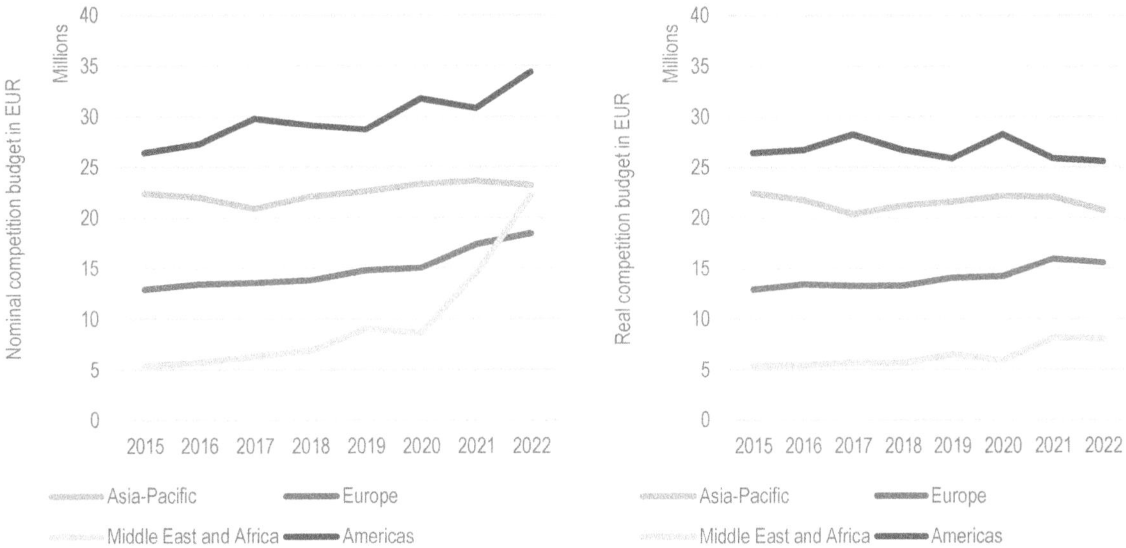

Note: Data based on the 64 jurisdictions in the OECD CompStats database that provided data for competition budget for eight years. Nominal and real competition budget figures are in 2015 euros (non-euro currencies are converted using 2015 official exchange rates on 31 December 2015) to eliminate distortions due to currency fluctuations. Inflation rates from all jurisdictions are taken from the World Bank development indicators database.
Source: OECD CompStats database.

StatLink https://stat.link/k95ovr

Figure 2.3. Average annual percentage growth in nominal (left) and real (right) competition budget (euros), by region, 2015-22

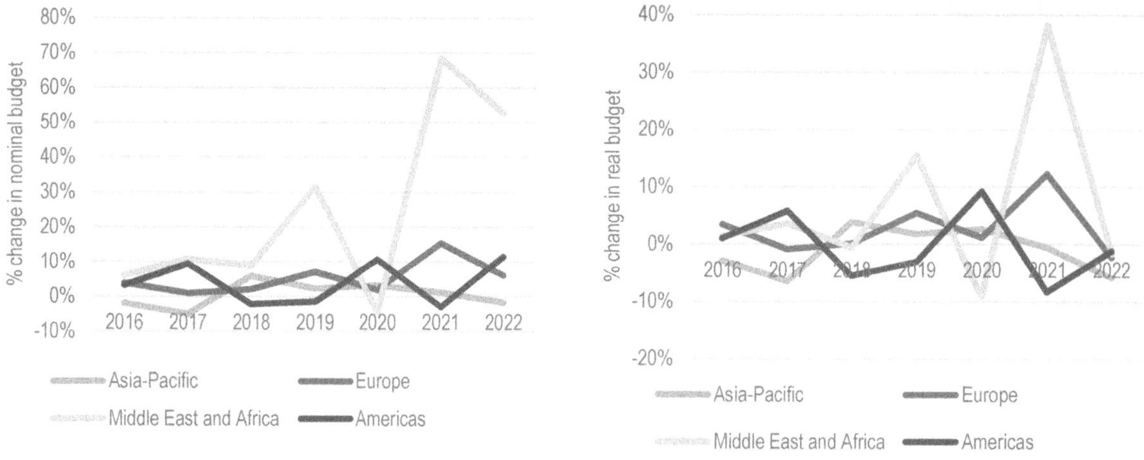

Note: Data based on the 64 jurisdictions in the OECD CompStats database that provided data for competition budget for eight years.
Source: OECD CompStats database.

StatLink https://stat.link/z1emwk

Cartel enforcement

Cartel leniency applications increased, similar to cartel ex-officio investigations

For the first time since 2015, when the OECD began collecting the Competition Statistics data, cases with leniency applications increased in all regions (from 10 cases with leniency applications in 2021 to 13 in 2022 in the Americas, 97 to 131 in Asia-Pacific, 86 to 92 in Europe, and 8 to 12 in MEA). The resurgence began in 2021 in Europe, continuing in 2022, and was accompanied by an increase in all three other regions. The total number of leniency applications increased from 201 in 2021 to 248 in 2022, an annual growth rate of 23.4%.

Notwithstanding the promising development of increasing leniency applications across all regions, the number of cases with applications remains significantly below levels in 2015 (more than 56% lower). Moreover, the increase is quite concentrated in a few jurisdictions. Even though 24 jurisdictions (45% of the 53 jurisdictions that provided data for this variable) saw an annual increase in leniency applications in 2022, four jurisdictions were responsible for most of the increase. One jurisdiction had an increase of 31 leniency applications in 2022, one an increase of 13, and two an increase of 7 leniency applications each. Finally, 16 jurisdictions (30%) had no change, while 13 jurisdictions (25%) had a decline in leniency applications.

Figure 2.4. Total leniency applications, by region, 2015-22

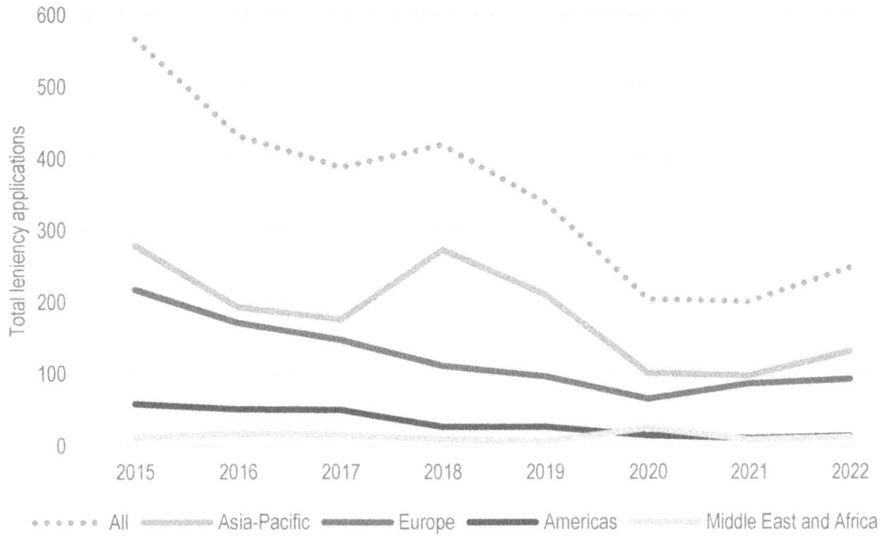

Note: Data based on the 53 jurisdictions in the OECD CompStats database that provided data for leniency applications for eight years.
Source: OECD CompStats database.

StatLink https://stat.link/vwh1fg

Cartel ex-officio investigations increased significantly in 2022 relative to 2021, countering the steady decline from 2016 to 2021. The average number of cartel ex-officio investigations launched per jurisdiction in 2022 was 8.4, up from 7.1 in 2021 (an annual growth of 19.3%).

Figure 2.5. Average cartel ex-officio investigations, 2015-22

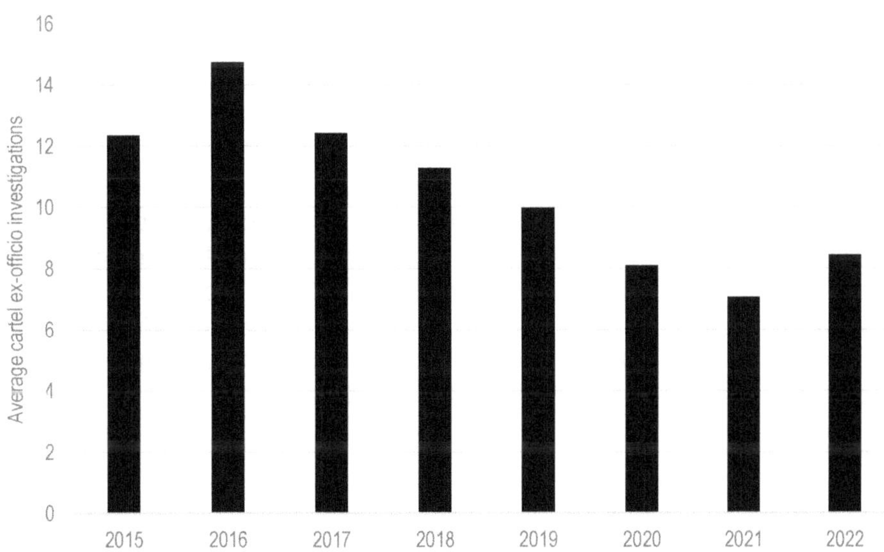

Note: Data based on the 60 jurisdictions in the OECD CompStats database that provided data for cartel ex-officio investigations for eight years.
Source: OECD CompStats database.

StatLink https://stat.link/t5o06f

Cartel dawn raids remained stable

The average number of cartel dawn raids remained stable in 2022 (with an average across all jurisdictions of 3.6 per jurisdiction in 2022), slightly increasing in Americas and Europe, while decreasing in Asia-Pacific and MEA.

Figure 2.6. Average number of cartel cases in which a dawn raid was carried out, by region, 2015-22

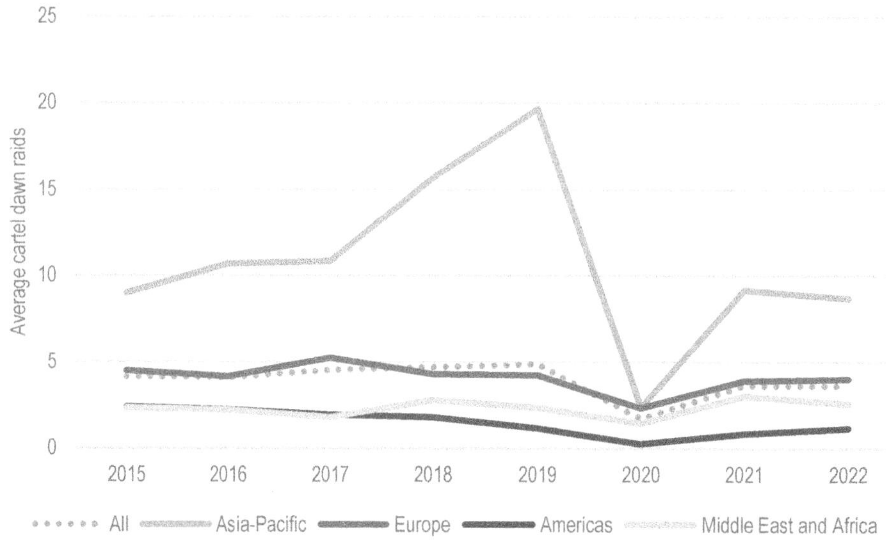

Note: Data based on the 56 jurisdictions in the OECD CompStats database that provided data for cartel dawn raids for eight years.
Source: OECD CompStats database.

StatLink https://stat.link/7f2xrd

Cartel decisions declined in Europe and MEA, but increased in Asia-Pacific and the Americas

In 2022, there was a decline in the number of cartel decisions in Europe and MEA, while the average number of decisions increased in Americas and Asia-Pacific. In Europe, the average number of cartel decisions decreased to 3.8, even below the value of 4.1 in 2020, while the average has been relatively stable around 5 decisions per jurisdiction over the period 2015 to 2021 (excluding 2020). In aggregate, this meant there was a decline in the average number of cartel decisions across all jurisdictions to 6.3 in 2022 from 6.8 in 2021, as well as in OECD and non-OECD jurisdictions (with the biggest decline of -13.9% in non-OECD jurisdictions, relative to only -3.7% in OECD jurisdictions).

Figure 2.7. Average number of cartel decisions, by region, 2015-22

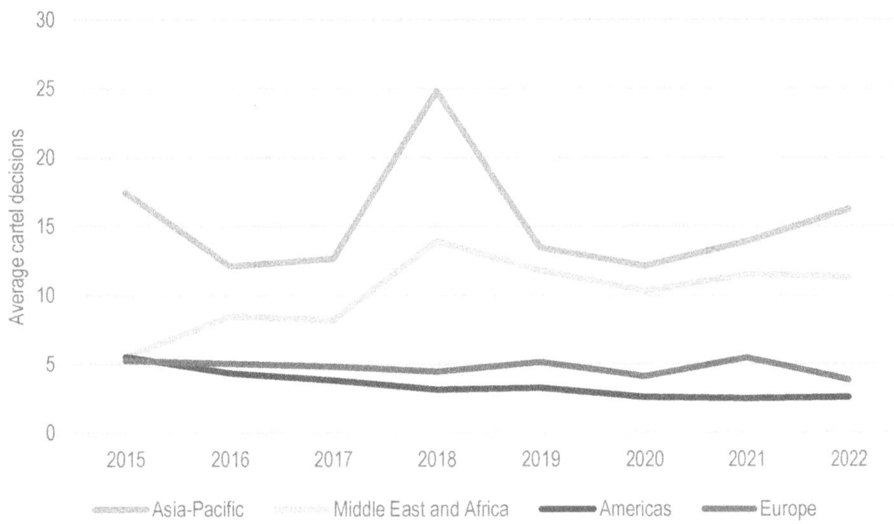

Note: Data based on the 68 jurisdictions in the OECD CompStats database that provided data for cartel decisions for eight years.
Source: OECD CompStats database.

StatLink https://stat.link/sv4bu6

Cartel bid-rigging decisions increased overall

There was an increase in bid-rigging cases across most jurisdictions between 2021 and 2022 (the only two years for which OECD CompStats data exists). The average number of bid-rigging decisions across all jurisdictions went from 2.2 in 2021 to 2.4 in 2022, an increase of 9.7%. As shown in Figure 2.8, bid-rigging cartel decisions in MEA and Americas increased in 2022, while decisions decreased in Europe and Asia-Pacific. The relative order of regions remained unchanged though, with Asia-Pacific having by far the highest number of bid-rigging cartel decisions per jurisdiction and MEA steadily catching up.

As a percentage of all cartel decisions, bid-rigging decisions across all jurisdictions increased from 32% in 2021 to 38% in 2022. In the Americas, MEA and Europe, bid-rigging cartel decisions increased as a share of all cartel decisions, although in Europe this is a reflection of the decrease in total cartel decisions.

Figure 2.8. Average number of cartel bid-rigging decisions (left) and percentage of all cartel decisions that are bid-rigging decisions (right), by region, 2021 and 2022

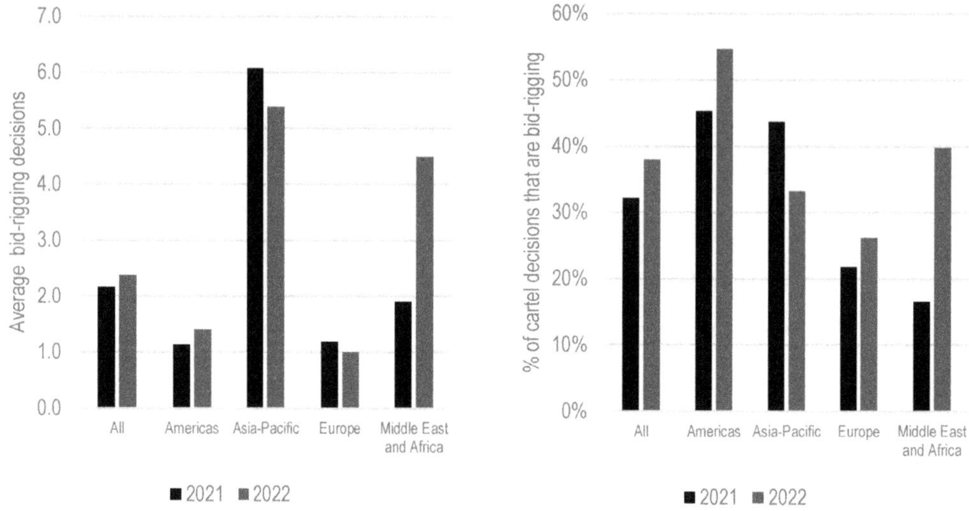

Note: Data based on the 71 jurisdictions in the OECD CompStats database that provided data for cartel bid-rigging decisions for 2021 and 2022.
Source: OECD CompStats database.

StatLink https://stat.link/9jt8a6

Cartel decisions by industry: Manufacturing, Construction and Wholesale Trade were still the industries with most cartel decisions

The top-10 industries based on the total number of cartel decisions remained relatively similar to the ranking in 2021, although there were some changes in 2022. "Manufacturing", "Construction" and "Wholesale Trade" remained the three industries with the most cartel decisions in 2022. They represented 44% of all cartel decisions in 2022, down from 48% in 2021. The biggest percentage decline from these three sectors was for "Wholesale Trade" with a decrease in participation of more than 40%.

Figure 2.9. Top-10 industries with cartel decisions in 2021 and 2022 as a percentage of all cartel decisions

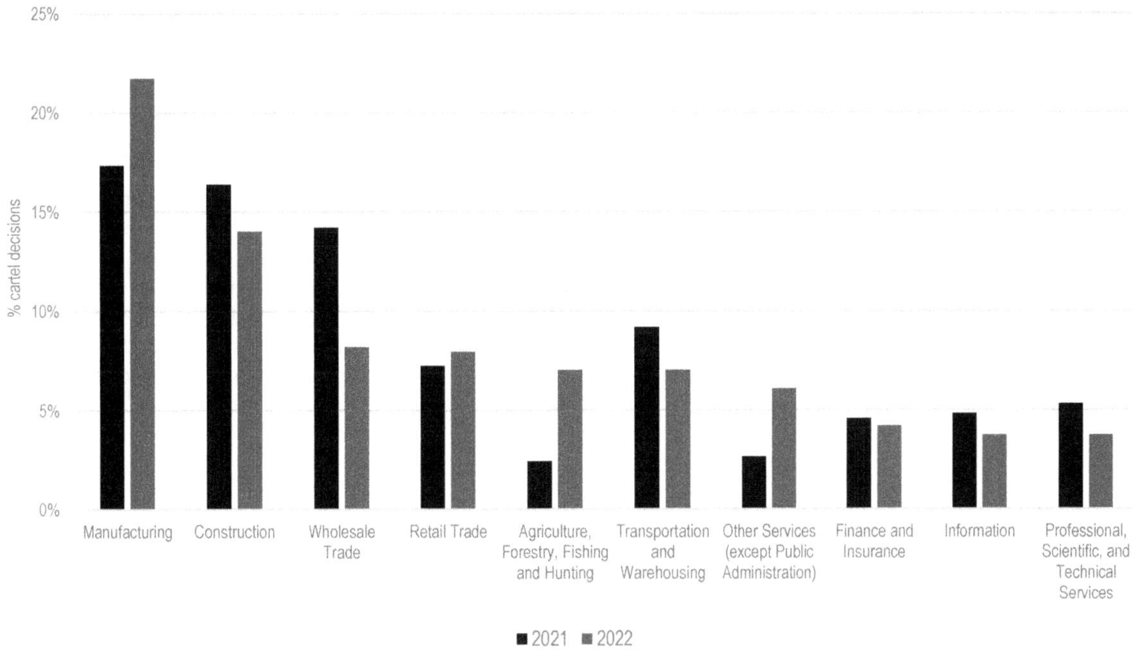

Note: Decisions by industry were classified according to two-digit NAICS codes. Their correspondence with the legends in this graph is as follows: 11 – agriculture, forestry, fishing and hunting, 21 – mining, quarrying, and oil and gas extraction, 22 – utilities, 23 – construction, 31-33 – manufacturing, 42 – wholesale trade, 44-45 – retail trade, 48-49 – transportation and warehousing, 51 – information, 52 – finance and insurance, 53 – real estate and rental and leasing, 54 – professional, scientific, and technical enterprises, 55 – management of companies and enterprises, 56 – administrative and support and waste management and remediation services, 61 – educational services, 62 – health care and social assistance, 71 – arts, entertainment, and recreation, 72 – accommodation and food services, 81 – other services (except public administration), 92 – public administration. Data based on the 69 jurisdictions in the OECD CompStats database that provided comparable data for 2021 and 2022.
Source: OECD CompStats database.

StatLink https://stat.link/v7jcl9

Table 2.1. Total cartel decisions by industry, 2021 and 2022

Rank 2022	Rank 2021	Sector	Total decisions 2021	Total decisions 2022
1	1	Manufacturing	72	93
2	2	Construction	68	60
3	3	Wholesale Trade	59	35
4	5	Retail Trade	30	34
5	12	Agriculture, Forestry, Fishing and Hunting	10	30
6	4	Transportation and Warehousing	38	30
7	11	Other Services (except Public Administration)	11	26
8	8	Finance and Insurance	19	18
9	7	Information	20	16
10	6	Professional, Scientific, and Technical Services	22	16
11	9	Administrative and Support and Waste Management and Remediation Services	16	16
12	10	Health Care and Social Assisstance	13	14
13	18	Arts, Entertainment, and Recreation	3	9
14	14	Real Estate Rental and Leasing	7	8

Rank 2022	Rank 2021	Sector	Total decisions 2021	Total decisions 2022
15	17	Public Administration	5	6
16	16	Utilities	5	5
17	13	Accommodation and Food Services	7	5
18	19	Mining, Quarrying, and Oil and Gas Extraction	3	3
19	15	Educational Services	6	3
20	20	Management of Companies and Enterprises	1	1

Note: Decisions by industry were classified according to two-digit NAICS codes. Their correspondence with the legends in this graph is as follows: 11 – agriculture, forestry, fishing and hunting, 21 – mining, quarrying, and oil and gas extraction, 22 – utilities, 23 – construction, 31-33 – manufacturing, 42 – wholesale trade, 44-45 – retail trade, 48-49 – transportation and warehousing, 51 – information, 52 – finance and insurance, 53 – real estate and rental and leasing, 54 – professional, scientific, and technical enterprises, 55 – management of companies and enterprises, 56 – administrative and support and waste management and remediation services, 61 – educational services, 62 – health care and social assistance, 71 – arts, entertainment, and recreation, 72 – accommodation and food services, 81 – other services (except public administration), 92 – public administration. Data based on the 69 jurisdictions in the OECD CompStats database that provided comparable data for 2021 and 2022.
Source: OECD CompStats database.

Cartel settlements were relatively stable

The average number of cartel cases with settlements was relatively stable in 2022, albeit with regional differences.

Across all jurisdictions, the number of cases in which settlements or plea bargain procedures for settling cartel infringement cases were used stayed relatively steady around 1.8 per jurisdiction on average. However, regional differences exist. The number of cases slightly increased in Asia-Pacific, while they strongly decreased in in MEA (from 4.3 in 2021 to 2.9 in 2022) and were relatively stable in Europe and the Americas.

Figure 2.10. Average number of cartel cases in which settlements or plea bargain procedures for settling infringement cases were used, by region, 2015-22

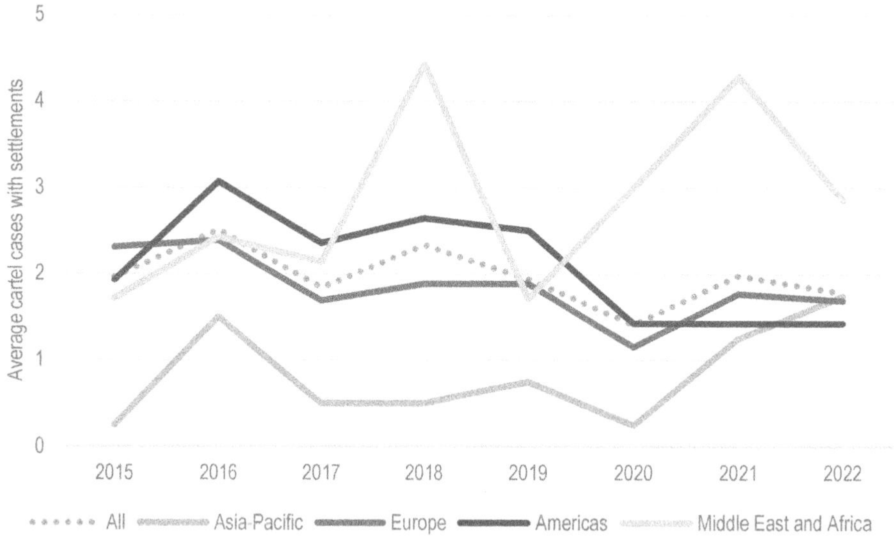

Note: Data based on the 51 jurisdictions in the OECD CompStats database that provided data for cartel settlements for eight years.
Source: OECD CompStats database.

StatLink https://stat.link/6vnw53

Abuse of dominance enforcement

Abuse of dominance investigations launched declined considerably

The average number of abuse of dominance investigations launched by competition authorities declined in all regions, except MEA. In 50 out of 63 jurisdictions with relevant data for all years, the number of investigations launched declined or remained unchanged. The average number of investigations launched was down from 5.6 in 2021 to 4.2 in 2022 across all jurisdictions, a decline of around 25%. While investigations launched were relatively stable between 2017 and 2021, the overall trend since 2016 shows a decline.

Figure 2.11. Average number of abuse of dominance investigations launched by the competition authority, 2015-22

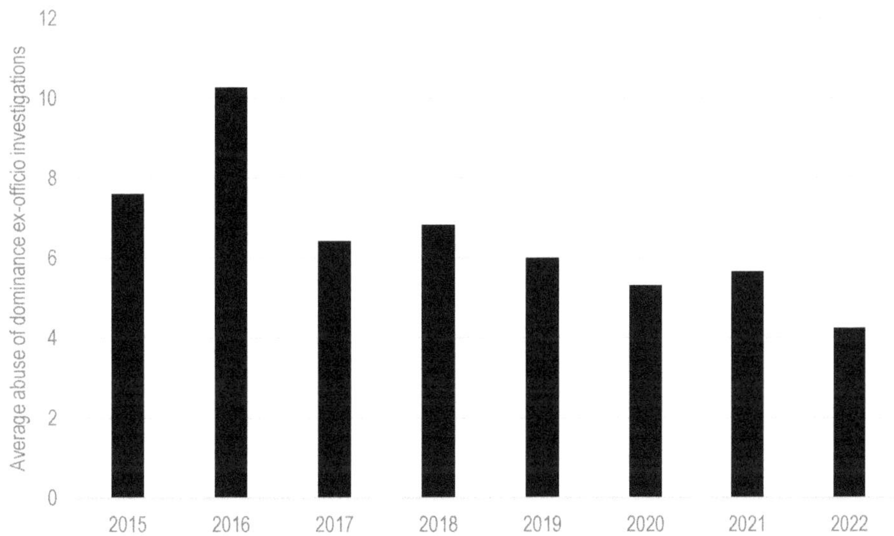

Note: Data based on the 63 jurisdictions in the OECD CompStats database that provided data for abuse of dominance investigations for eight years. This is the number of separate cases, not the number of companies involved.
Source: OECD CompStats database.

StatLink https://stat.link/yjwsh0

Abuse of dominance dawn raids increased in the Americas and MEA, but decreased in Europe

The use of dawn raids for abuse of dominance cases remains fairly scarce. They increased in the Americas and MEA (albeit from very low values, particularly in the Americas). Most abuse of dominance dawn raids occur in MEA, where the average number per jurisdiction went from 0.5 in 2021 to 1.28 dawn raids in 2022, even though it was driven by a single jurisdiction. In Europe, there was a considerable decline in 2022, all driven by a few jurisdictions, although the movements tend to be quite erratic over the full period (2015-22), and the average value of 0.56 per jurisdiction (across all jurisdictions in 2022) is low in any case. Of the jurisdictions that provided data, most did not perform any dawn raids for abuse of dominance cases in 2022. In Asia-Pacific there have not been any abuse of dominance dawn raids since 2017.

Figure 2.12. Average number of abuse of dominance cases in which a dawn raid was carried out, by region, 2015-22

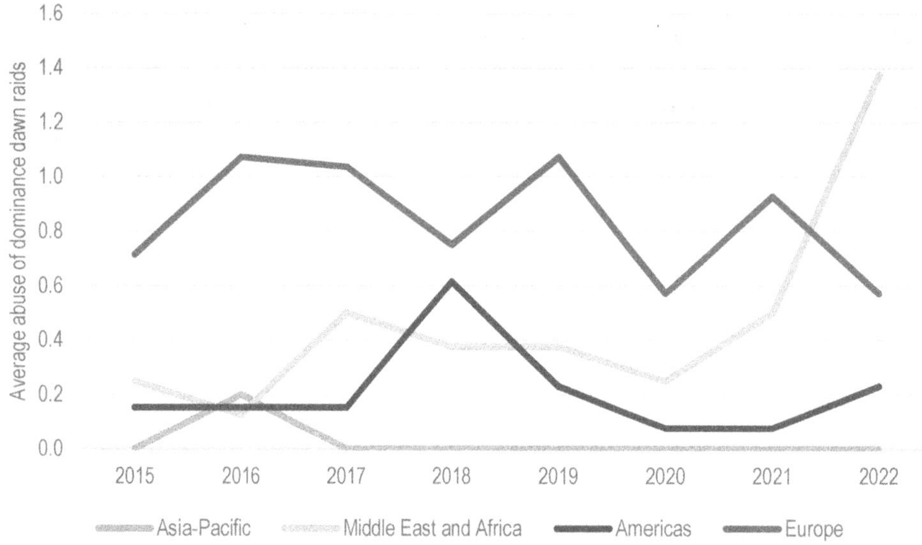

Note: Data based on the 54 jurisdictions in the OECD CompStats database that provided data for abuse of dominance dawn raids for eight years. This is the number of separate cases, not the number of companies involved.
Source: OECD CompStats database.

StatLink https://stat.link/t6ap1q

Abuse of dominance decisions declined overall, continuing a broader trend since 2015

The average number of dominance decisions declined significantly, decreasing from 2 in 2021 to 1.5 in 2022. This continues a slow downward trend over the period, from an average of 2.4 abuse of dominance decisions per jurisdiction in 2015 to 1.5 in 2022. For both OECD and non-OECD jurisdictions, the average abuse of dominance decisions declined considerably in 2022 by 30% and 21%, respectively. This decrease reverts the growth of abuse of dominance decisions in these regions witnessed between 2020 and 2021.

Figure 2.13. Average number of abuse of dominance decisions taken by the competition authority, 2015-22

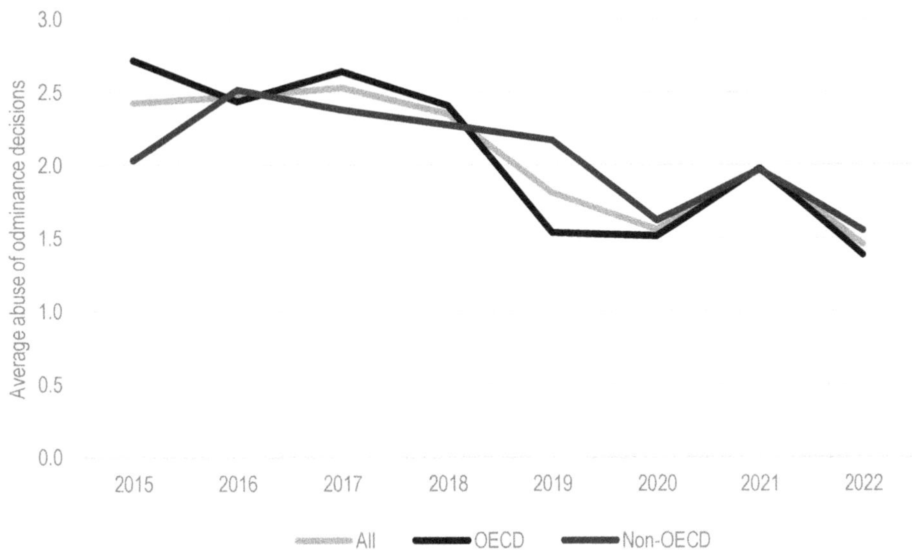

Note: Data based on the 68 jurisdictions in the OECD CompStats database that provided data for abuse of dominance decisions for eight years. This is the number of abuse of dominance decisions taken by the competition authority (or judgment by a relevant court, if "competition authority" is not applicable because the competition authority does not take decisions in your jurisdiction).
Source: OECD CompStats database.

StatLink https://stat.link/ib0e2c

Abuse of dominance decisions by industry: Transportation & Warehousing, Manufacturing and Information were still the industries with the most abuse of dominance decisions

The top 10 industries based on the total number of abuse of dominance decisions in 2022 was similar to 2021. "Transportation and Warehousing", "Manufacturing" and "Information" remained the three industries with the most abuse of dominance decisions in 2022. They represented 47% of all abuse of dominance decisions in 2022, the same proportion as in 2021.

Figure 2.14. Top-10 industries with abuse of dominance decisions in 2021 and 2022 as a percentage of all abuse of dominance decisions

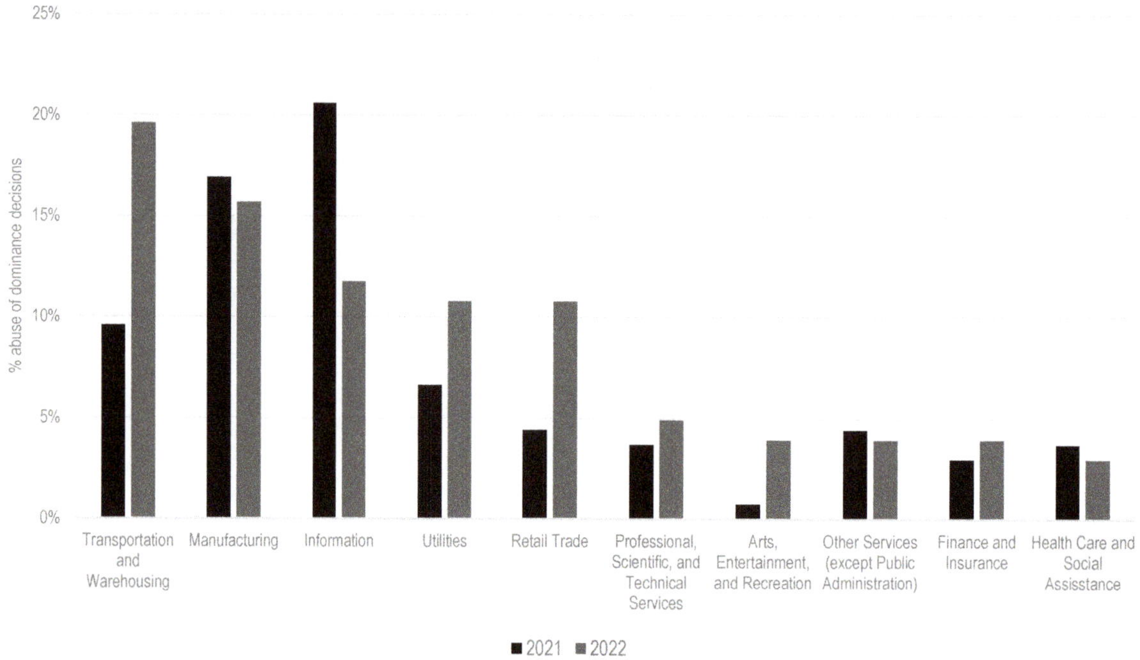

Note: Decisions by industry were classified according to two-digit NAICS codes. Their correspondence with the legends in this graph is as follows: 11 – agriculture, forestry, fishing and hunting, 21 – mining, quarrying, and oil and gas extraction, 22 – utilities, 23 – construction, 31-33 – manufacturing, 42 – wholesale trade, 44-45 – retail trade, 48-49 – transportation and warehousing, 51 – information, 52 – finance and insurance, 53 – real estate and rental and leasing, 54 – professional, scientific, and technical enterprises, 55 – management of companies and enterprises, 56 – administrative and support and waste management and remediation services, 61 – educational services, 62 – health care and social assistance, 71 – arts, entertainment, and recreation, 72 – accommodation and food services, 81 – other services (except public administration), 92 – public administration. Data based on the 71 jurisdictions in the OECD CompStats database that provided comparable data for 2021 and 2022.
Source: OECD CompStats database.

StatLink https://stat.link/oh4s5w

Table 2.2. Total abuse of dominance decisions by industry, 2021 and 2022

Rank 2022	Rank 2021	Sector	Total decisions 2021	Total decisions 2022
1	3	Transportation and Warehousing	13	20
2	2	Manufacturing	23	16
3	1	Information	28	12
4	5	Utilities	9	11
5	7	Retail Trade	6	11
6	9	Professional, Scientific, and Technical Services	5	5
7	17	Arts, Entertainment, and Recreation	1	4
8	8	Other Services (except Public Administration)	6	4
9	11	Finance and Insurance	4	4
10	10	Health Care and Social Assisstance	5	3
11	4	Wholesale Trade	13	3
12	15	Accommodation and Food Services	3	3
13	12	Administrative and Support and Waste Management and Remediation Services	3	3
14	14	Construction	3	1

Rank 2022	Rank 2021	Sector	Total decisions 2021	Total decisions 2022
15	13	Public Administration	3	1
16	6	Agriculture, Forestry, Fishing and Hunting	7	1
17	16	Mining, Quarrying, and Oil and Gas Extraction	2	0
18	18	Management of Companies and Enterprises	1	0
19	19	Real Estate Rental and Leasing	1	0
20	20	Educational Services	0	0

Note: Decisions by industry were classified according to two-digit NAICS codes. Their correspondence with the legends in this graph is as follows: 11 – agriculture, forestry, fishing and hunting, 21 – mining, quarrying, and oil and gas extraction, 22 – utilities, 23 – construction, 31-33 – manufacturing, 42 – wholesale trade, 44-45 – retail trade, 48-49 – transportation and warehousing, 51 – information, 52 – finance and insurance, 53 – real estate and rental and leasing, 54 – professional, scientific, and technical enterprises, 55 – management of companies and enterprises, 56 – administrative and support and waste management and remediation services, 61 – educational services, 62 – health care and social assistance, 71 – arts, entertainment, and recreation, 72 – accommodation and food services, 81 – other services (except public administration), 92 – public administration. Data based on the 71 jurisdictions in the OECD CompStats database that provided comparable data for 2021 and 2022.
Source: OECD CompStats database.

Abuse of dominance settlements and commitment decisions declined, mostly driven by the Americas

Few abuse of dominance cases are solved by a way of a settlement or a commitment. In 2022, the use of both figures further declined. The average number of abuse of dominance cases in which settlements or plea bargain procedures for settling infringement cases were used slightly declined in 2022, although this was mostly driven by the Americas and Asia-Pacific. In fact, in Asia-Pacific, no abuse of dominance cases were settled in 2022. Their use increased somewhat in Europe and MEA, although their use of settlements for abuse of dominance cases also remains limited (0.2 and 0.9, respectively).

Figure 2.15. Average number of abuse of dominance cases in which settlements or plea bargain procedures for settling infringement cases were used, by region, 2021-22

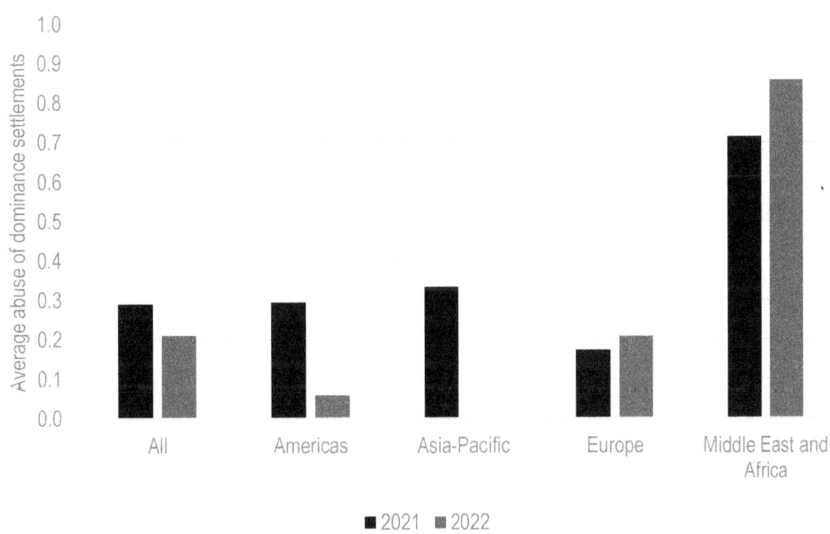

Note: Data based on the 62 jurisdictions in the OECD CompStats database that provided data for abuse of dominance settlements for eight years.
Source: OECD CompStats database.

StatLink https://stat.link/k4v3jg

Figure 2.16. Average number of abuse of dominance cases in which commitment procedures or other types of negotiated/consensual procedures were used, by region, 2021-22

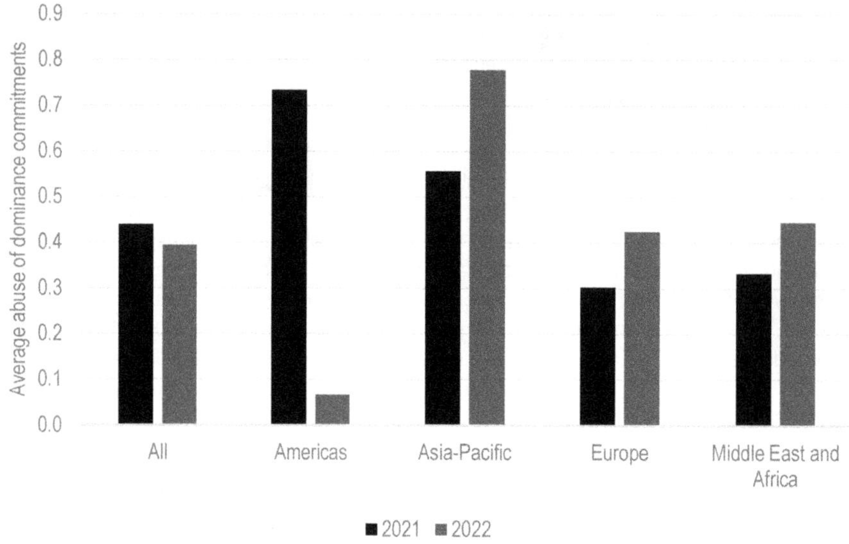

Note: Data based on the 66 jurisdictions in the OECD CompStats database that provided data for abuse of dominance commitment decisions for eight years.
Source: OECD CompStats database.

StatLink https://stat.link/fxj1hi

Sanctions

Overall cartel and abuse of dominance fines decreased

Fines for both cartels and abuse of dominance cases declined in 2022. The average abuse of dominance fines imposed per jurisdiction declined 52% from 42.5 million euros in 2021 to 20.4 million euros in 2022. The average amount of cartel fines imposed per jurisdiction decreased 45% from 89.8 million euros in 2021 to 49.5 million euros in 2022. As in most years, there were more fines for cartel infringements than abuse of dominance cases. The amount of fines imposed is erratic in most jurisdictions, without a clear trend and can vary considerably from year to year, particularly for abuse of dominance fines (which peaked in 2018). Cartel fines are more consistent over the period, with an average of around 82 million euros per jurisdiction across the period 2015 to 2022.

Figure 2.17. Average fines imposed per jurisdiction by type of infringement (cartel cases and abuse of dominance cases), 2015-22

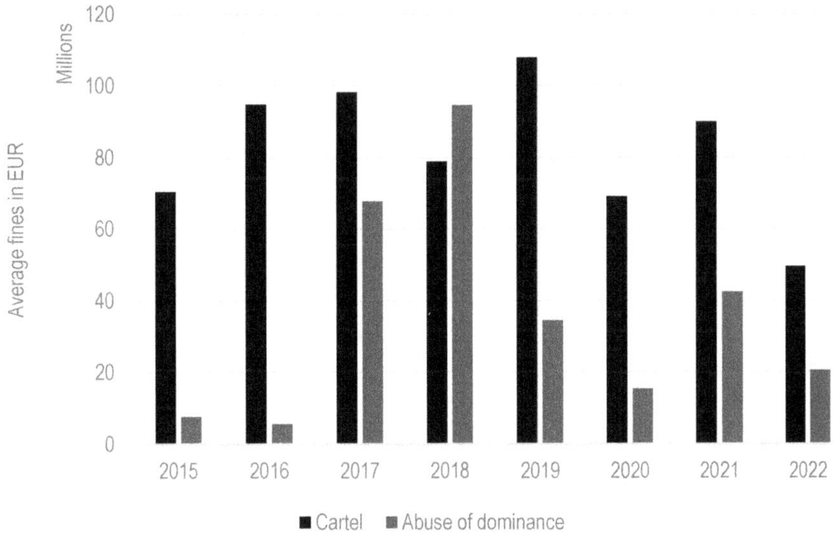

Note: Data based on the 66 (for cartel) and 64 (for abuse of dominance) jurisdictions in the OECD CompStats database that provided data for cartel and abuse of dominance fines for eight years. Nominal fines imposed are in 2015 euros (non-euro currencies are converted using 2015 official exchange rates on 31 December 2015) to eliminate distortions due to currency fluctuations.
Source: OECD CompStats database.

StatLink https://stat.link/sqtl14

The value of the total cartel fines imposed in 2022 was EUR 3.27 billion while the total abuse of dominance fines imposed was 1.31 billion. In Asia-Pacific, no fines on abuse of dominance were imposed in 2022.

Figure 2.18. Total fines imposed per jurisdiction in cartels (left) and abuse of dominance cases (right), by region, 2015-22

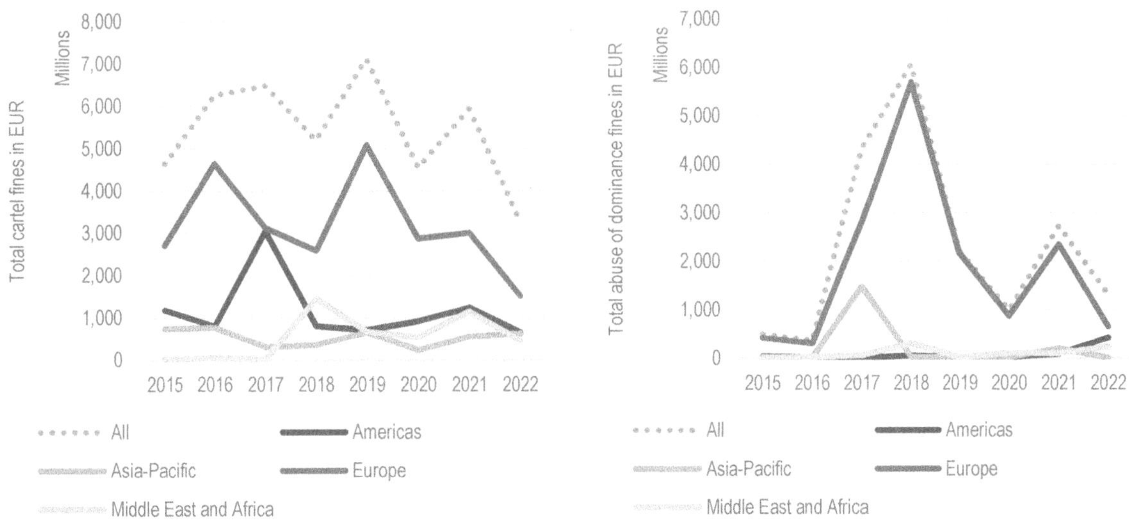

Note: Data based on the 66 (for cartel) and 64 (for abuse of dominance) jurisdictions in the OECD CompStats database that provided data for cartel and abuse of dominance fines for eight years. Nominal fines imposed are in 2015 euros (non-euro currencies are converted using 2015 official exchange rates on 31 December 2015) to eliminate distortions due to currency fluctuations.
Source: OECD CompStats database.

StatLink https://stat.link/m1g8pr

The number of companies fined increased for abuse of dominance, but remained relatively steady for cartels

The average number of companies fined per jurisdiction remained relatively steady at around 16 for cartels, while it increased for abuse of dominance in 2022 (close to 2, which is the highest since 2015).

Figure 2.19. Average number of companies fined per jurisdiction in cartel decisions (left) and abuse of dominance decisions (right), 2015-22

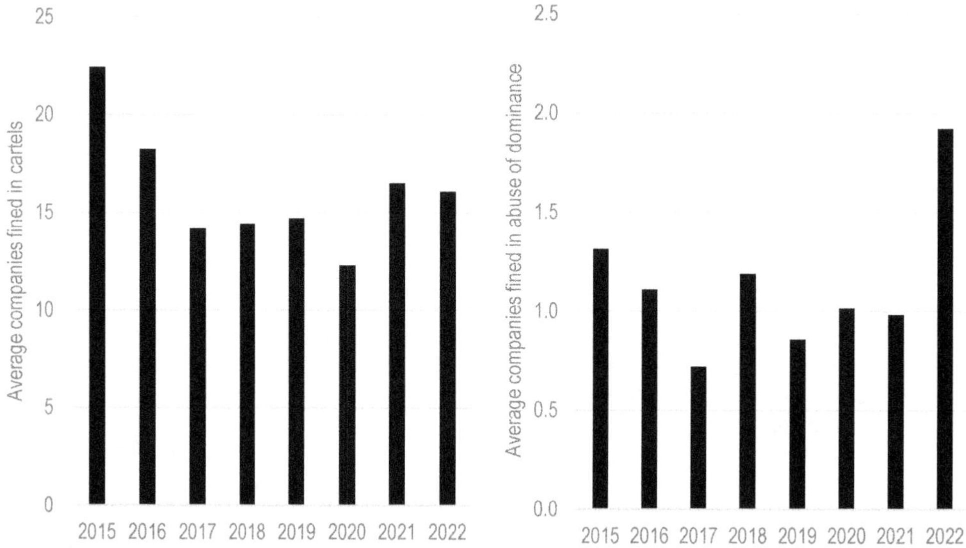

Note: Data based on the 66 jurisdictions (for cartels) and 64 jurisdictions (abuse of dominance) in the OECD CompStats database that provided data for companies fined for cartel and abuse of dominance for eight years.
Source: OECD CompStats database.

StatLink https://stat.link/pn2hzj

The number of cartel cases in which Individuals were fined was fairly low and decreasing

The average number of cartel cases in which individuals were fined in cartel cases was fairly erratic when considering given regions, however this averaged out over the period at around 2.9 cartel cases per jurisdiction in which a fine was imposed on an individual.

Figure 2.20. Average number of cartel cases in which fines on individuals were imposed by the competition authority or by a court (excluding appeals), by region, 2015-22

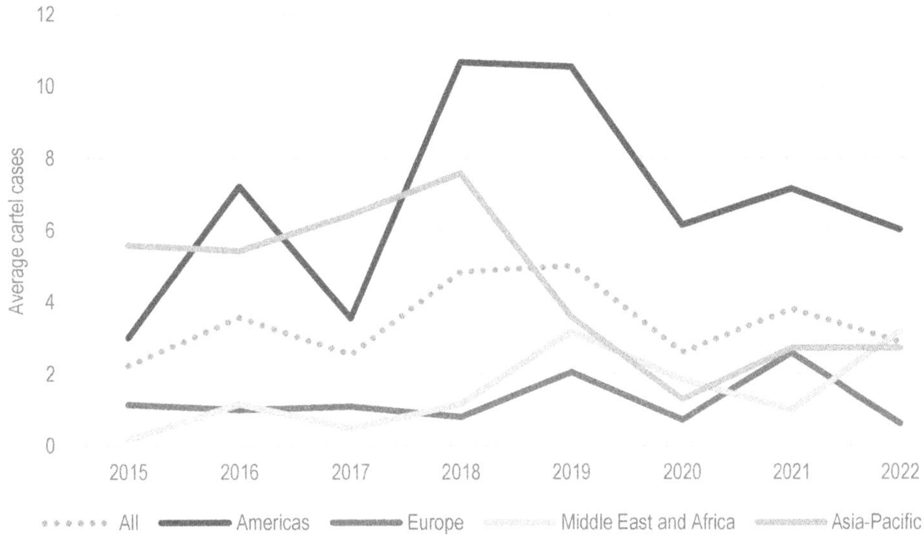

Note: Data based on the 49 jurisdictions in the OECD CompStats database that provided data for cartel cases in which fines on individuals were imposed for eight years.
Source: OECD CompStats database.

StatLink https://stat.link/3nwpxy

Advocacy

Market studies increased in most regions

The average number of market studies per jurisdiction was relatively stable in all regions, except Asia-Pacific where it increased considerably. In Asia-Pacific, the average per jurisdiction increased from 3.2 in 2021 to 5.4 in 2022 (growth of 65%) market studies per authority. However, this is mostly driven by a handful of jurisdictions in the region. In general, the most relevant increase came from non-OECD jurisdictions (where the average went from 2.1 to 2.7 studies per year), as in OECD jurisdiction the average number remained the same (3 market studies per year).

Figure 2.21. Average number of market studies, by region, 2015-22

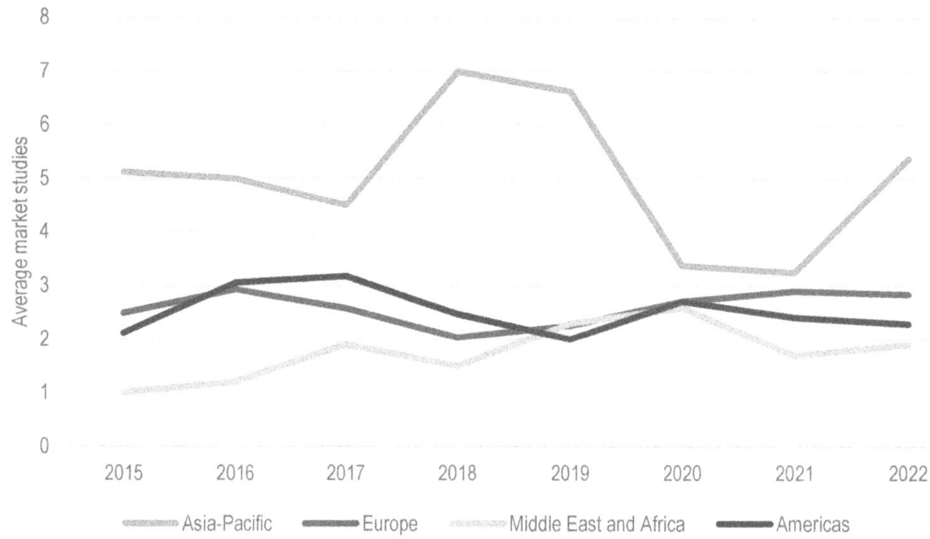

Note: Data based on the 66 jurisdictions in the OECD CompStats database that provided data for market studies for eight years.
Source: OECD CompStats database.

StatLink https://stat.link/eba8gz

3 In focus: trends in merger control

This chapter is dedicated to merger control, providing an analysis of: (i) the OECD CompStats merger data, which is now available publicly on an individualised basis, and thus can be explained in more detail than was previously possible; and (ii) a new dataset collected by the OECD Secretariat on all prohibition decisions over the period 2015 to 2022.

This year, for the first time, jurisdictions agreed to make public data on merger control on an individualised basis. With this in mind, this chapter presents trends in merger control on an aggregate basis, but explains which jurisdictions are driving these aggregate trends. Individualised merger control data can be found in the Excel file supporting this years' report.

Trends in CompStats merger control

Merger notifications declined in OECD jurisdictions

In 2022, there was a drop in the number of overall merger notifications. However, this was predominantly driven by a decline specifically in OECD jurisdictions. The number of merger notifications in non-OECD jurisdictions continued to increase in 2022, although at a slower rate than in 2021. Despite the decline in overall merger notifications in 2022, they were still higher than at any point in the period 2015 to 2020 (with an average of 179 per jurisdiction, which was above the previous peak of 154 in 2019).

Figure 3.1. Average number of merger notifications, 2015-22

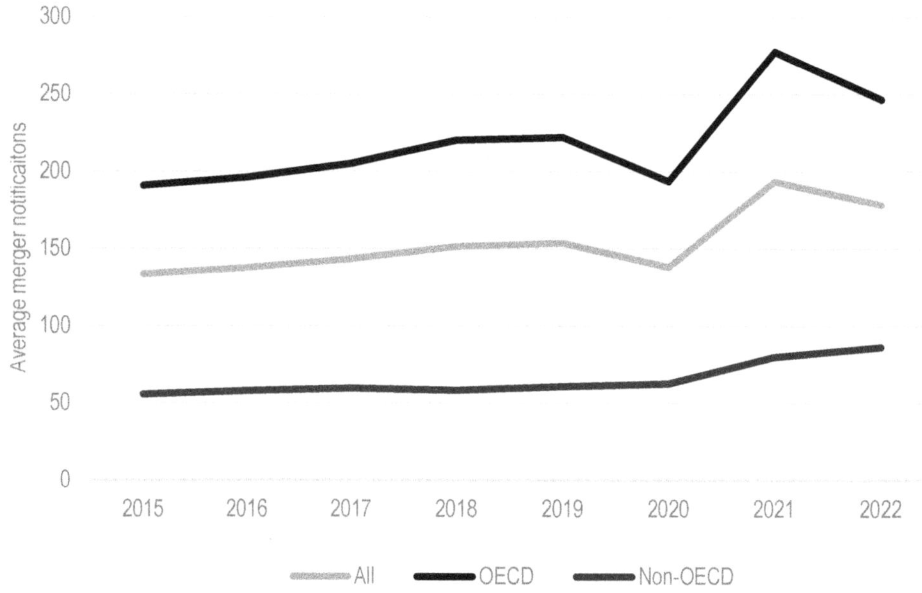

Note: Data based on the 66 jurisdictions in the OECD CompStats database that provided comparable data for all eight years.
Source: OECD CompStats database.

StatLink https://stat.link/riycu3

As shown in Figure 3.2, the decline in merger notifications in 2022 was common across most OECD jurisdictions with 63% of OECD jurisdictions (24 of 38 jurisdictions with relevant data for all years) observing a reduction in merger notifications, while notifications decreased in 36% (10 of 38 jurisdictions with relevant data for all years) of non-OECD jurisdictions. Furthermore, for jurisdictions that had positive percentage growth in 2022, it was much higher in non-OECD jurisdictions with an average of 47%, compared to only 26% in OECD jurisdictions. It is important to note than in the case of Peru, the percentage change is due to the extension of the merger control regime beyond the energy sector to all sectors of the economy.

The surge in merger notifications in 2021 was largely due to the significant increase in the US, from 1 580 merger notifications in 2020 to 3 413 merger notifications in 2021. However, in 2022, it decreased by 11% to 3 029 (although this value was still 92% higher than the number of merger notifications in 2020).

Figure 3.2. Distribution per jurisdiction of the percentage change in the number of merger notifications from 2021 to 2022, for OECD (left) and non-OECD jurisdictions (right)

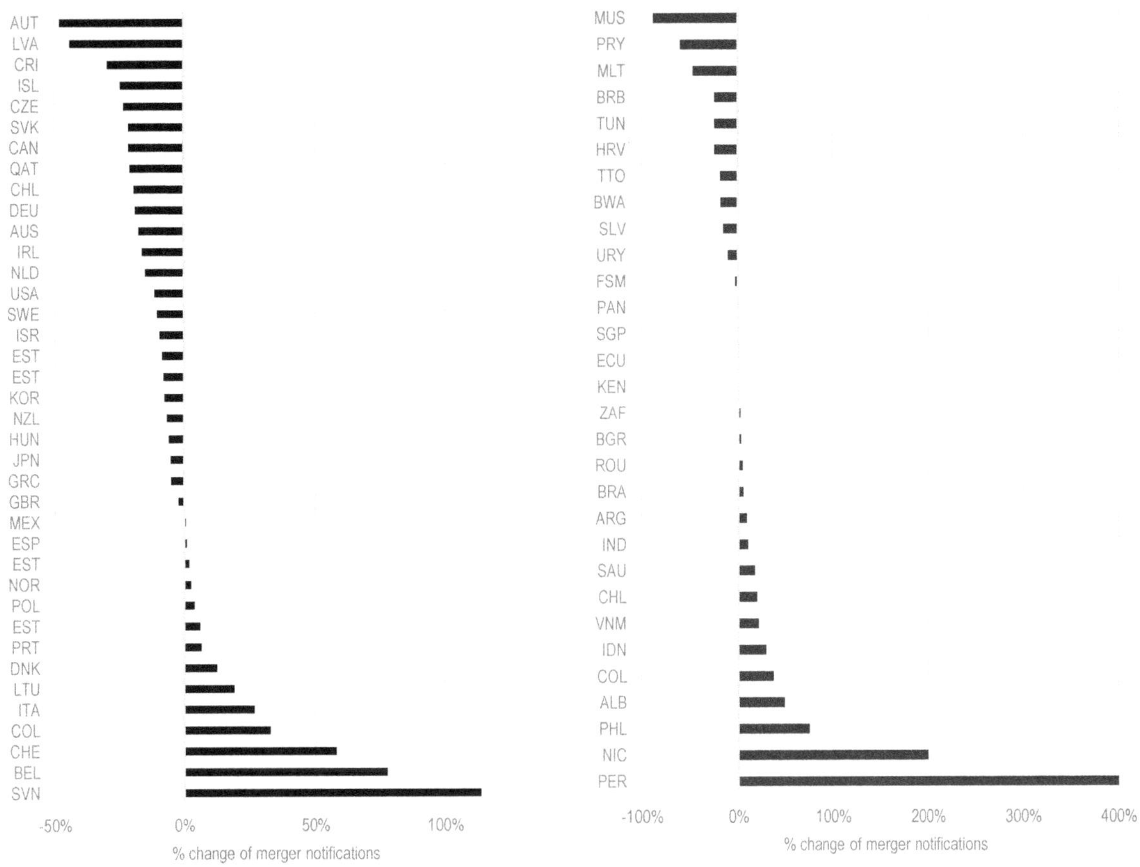

Note: Data based on the 68 jurisdictions in the OECD CompStats database that provided data for 2021 and 2022. Each bar represents one jurisdiction.
Source: OECD CompStats database.

StatLink https://stat.link/90jo5y

When looking at the merger notifications by region, the decline is observed in all of them. In Europe, merger notifications declined the most (12% compared to 2021), followed by the Americas (decline in 8%), MEA (decline in 5%) and Asia-Pacific (decline in 3%).

Figure 3.3. Average number of merger notifications by region, 2015-22

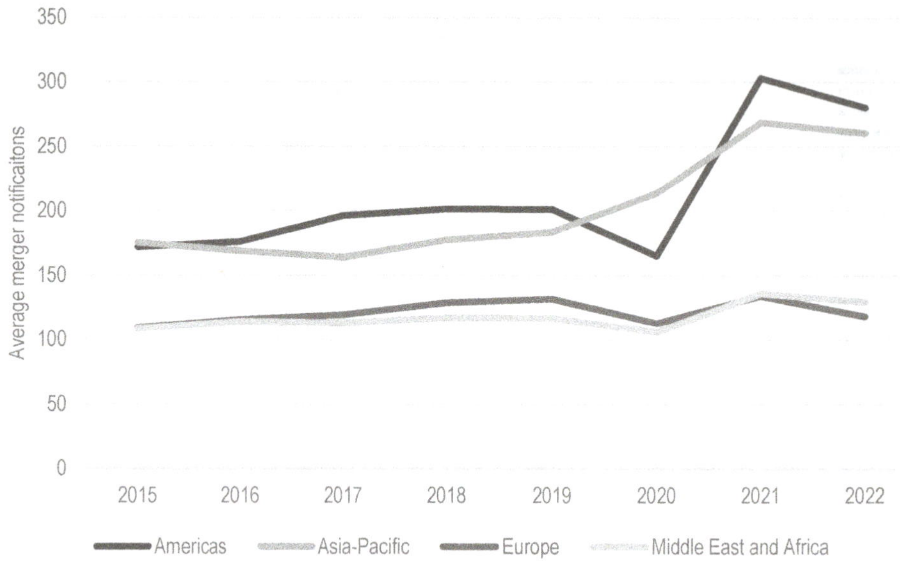

Note: Data based on the 66 jurisdictions in the OECD CompStats database that provided comparable data for all eight years.
Source: OECD CompStats database.

StatLink https://stat.link/trghy5

Merger intervention rate increased in OECD jurisdictions

Contrary to the previous year, there was a significant increase in the merger intervention rate – the proportion of transactions in which competition authorities intervened, either by imposing a remedy or by prohibiting a transaction – in 2022. This holds true regardless of whether withdrawn mergers are included in the numerator or not. Most of this increase was driven by OECD jurisdictions, while for non-OECD jurisdictions it remained stable.

The increase in 2022 observed in OECD jurisdictions was driven by the United Kingdom (15% in 2021 to 53% in 2022), Iceland (7% in 2021 to 30% in 2022), Greece (0% in 2021 to 10% in 2022), New Zealand (6% in 2021 to 13% in 2022) and Ireland (4% in 2021 to 10% in 2022).[2]

The downward decline in non-OECD jurisdictions between 2017 and 2021, was not driven by steady decline in any particular jurisdictions. The variation over time in these jurisdictions was more erratic, varying significantly from year to year. The merger intervention rate in non-OECD jurisdictions has been steadily declining from a peak of 8.1% in 2017 to a low of 4.3% in 2022.

The merger intervention rate was also declining in OECD jurisdictions over the period 2018 to 2021, however this trend was reversed in 2022, with a sharp increase. This increase in OECD jurisdictions was due to both: (i) an increase in the absolute number of merger decisions where the authority has intervened from 135 in 2021 to 173 in 2022 (i.e., increase in the numerator); and (ii) a decline in the number of overall decisions from 10 243 in 2021 to 9 026 in 2022 (i.e., decrease in the denominator).

Figure 3.4. Average merger intervention rate (excluding withdrawn mergers), 2015-22

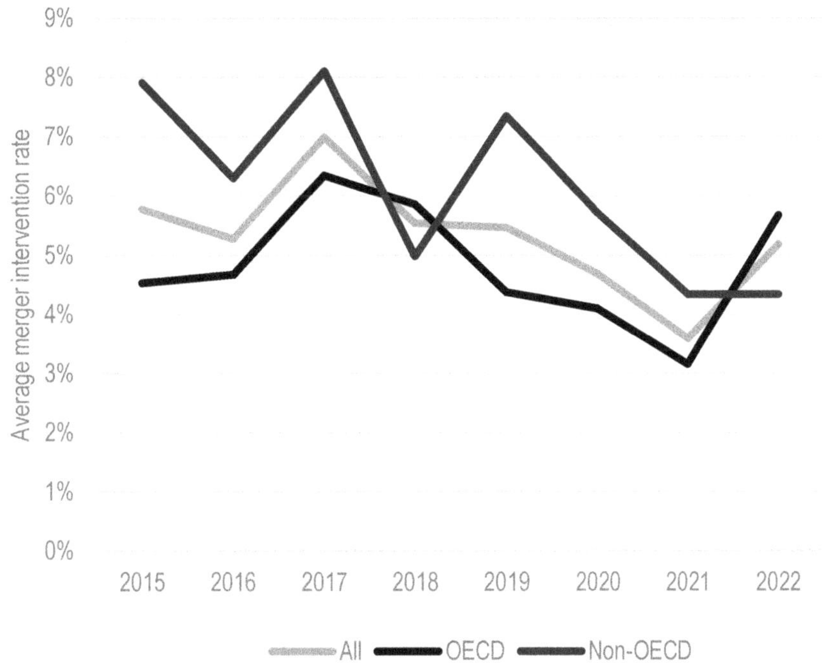

Note: Data based on the 60 jurisdictions in the OECD CompStats database that provided comparable data for all eight years.
Source: OECD CompStats database.

StatLink https://stat.link/ie1pqu

Regional differences in the evolution of the intervention rate exist. While it increased in Europe and MEA, it decreased in Asia-Pacific and Americas. MEA jurisdictions had the highest intervention rate in 2022, with an average of 7.3%, increasing from 5.9% in 2021. In Asia-Pacific, the intervention rate in 2022 was the lowest, with an average of only 2.7%, decreasing from 3.4% in 2021. In Europe, the intervention rate increased the most, from 2.8% in 2021 to 5.9% in 2022, while in the Americas, it decreased the most, from 4.5% in 2021 to 3.4% in 2022.

Figure 3.5. Average merger intervention rate (excluding withdrawn mergers) per region, 2015-22

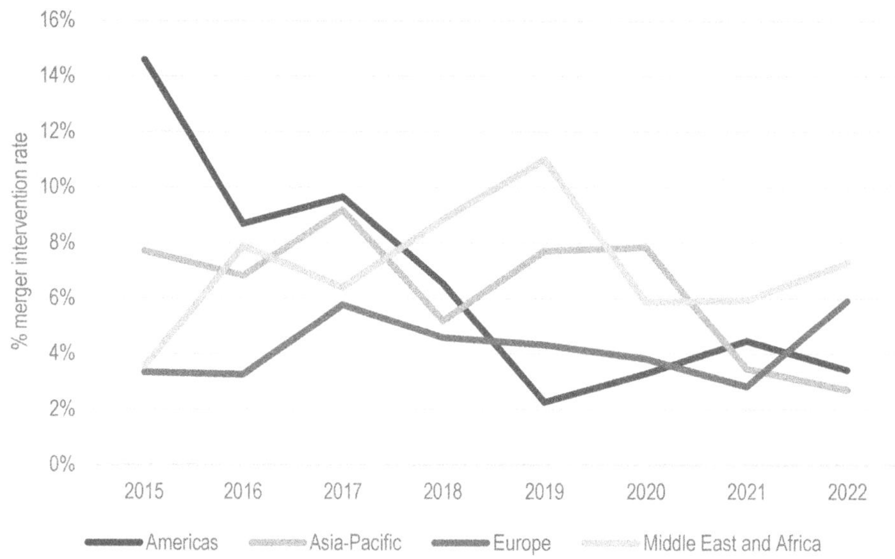

Note: Data based on the 60 jurisdictions in the OECD CompStats database that provided comparable data for all eight years.
Source: OECD CompStats database.

StatLink https://stat.link/uvogt6

Merger remedies were more frequently used by authorities

As shown in Figure 3.6, the increase of intervention rate in 2022 was mainly due to an increase in the use of remedies. This was both the use of remedies in phase II (increasing from 108 to 185) and in phase I (from 61 to 78). Prohibitions and withdrawn mergers were relatively similar in 2022 (34 and 53, respectively) compared to 2021 (29 and 49, respectively), meaning that they do not explain the increase in the intervention rate.

Figure 3.6. Number of merger decisions by outcome where an authority intervened or a merger was withdrawn, 2015-22

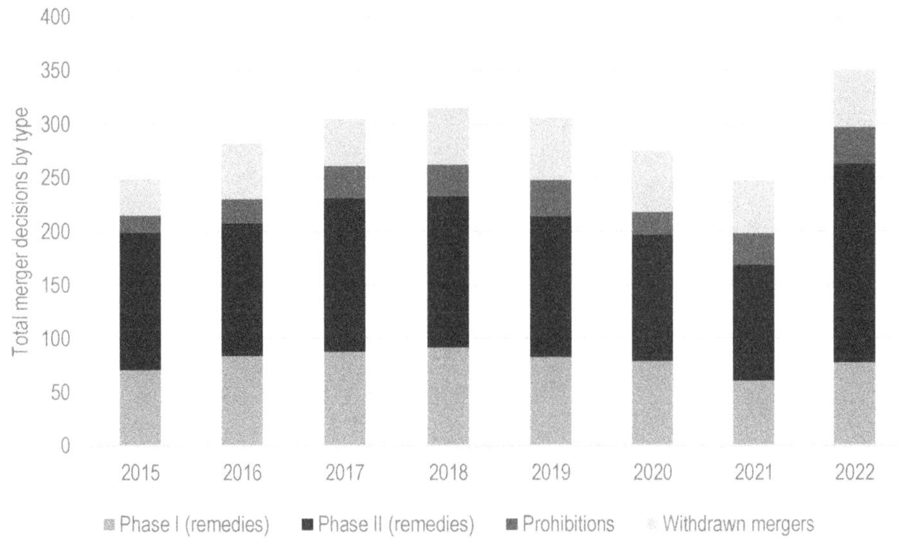

Note: Data based on the 66 jurisdictions in the OECD CompStats database that provided comparable data for all eight years.
Source: OECD CompStats database.

StatLink https://stat.link/z7ipyh

Trends in OECD prohibitions data

Most merger prohibitions are concentrated in a few jurisdictions

The OECD Secretariat gathered the decisions of all merger prohibitions identified by competition authorities in the Competition Statistics survey for the period 2015 to 2022. There were 216 prohibition decisions in total.

Based on a review of available prohibition decisions, competition authority websites and annual reports on the OECD website, the Secretariat created several additional variables, including: (i) theory of harm in which the authorities based their decisions (which consists of horizontal unilateral effects, horizontal coordinated effects, vertical effects, conglomerate effects and others); (ii) industry (based on the NAICS classification); and (iii) market. This section of the report provides a summary of those variables.

Most prohibitions are concentrated in a few jurisdictions. The six jurisdictions with the most prohibitions represent 57% of all prohibitions during the period 2015 to 2022 (124 of 216 prohibitions). They are South Africa, United States, United Kingdom, Israel, Germany and the European Union.

Figure 3.7. Total prohibitions, by jurisdiction, 2015-2022

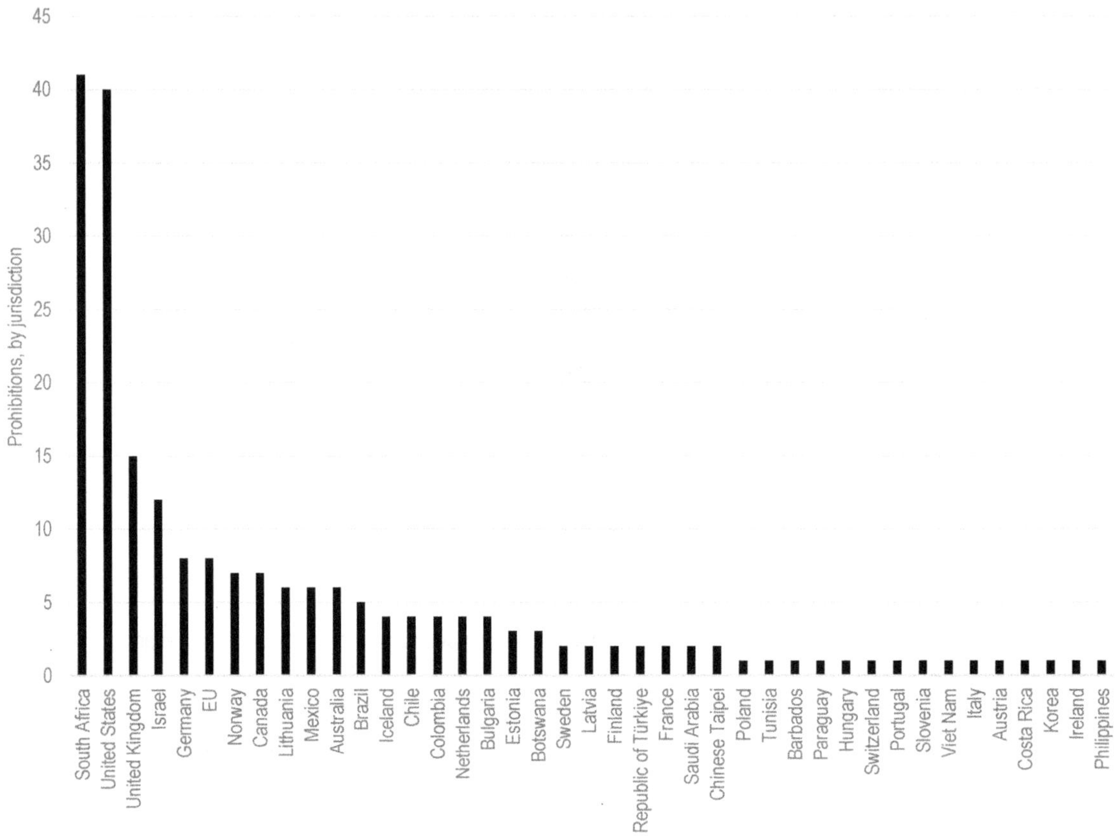

Note: Data based on the 66 jurisdictions in the OECD CompStats database.
Source: OECD CompStats database.

StatLink https://stat.link/i5a36h

Most prohibitions rely on horizontal theories of harm

Horizontal theories of harm make up the vast majority in merger prohibition decisions (173 decisions). Horizontal coordinated theories of harm (36 decisions) are similar in amount to vertical theories of harm (39 decisions). Conglomerate theories of harm are negligible in merger prohibition decisions (only 4 decisions). There are also some jurisdictions that have other theories of harm, such as public interest theories of harm in South Africa (although these are not included in the figure below).

Several prohibitions considered multiple theories of harm in the decision, especially in cases where horizontal unilateral effects were not the main concern. While only 20% of the mergers that were prohibited as a result of horizontal unilateral concerns also considered another theory of harm, this proportion increases significantly when looking at mergers prohibited for coordinated and vertical effects (56% and 59% of the cases, respectively). All prohibitions that considered conglomerate effects also included another theory of harm.

Figure 3.8. Total prohibitions, by theory of harm and whether it relied on a single or multiple theories of harm, 2015-2022

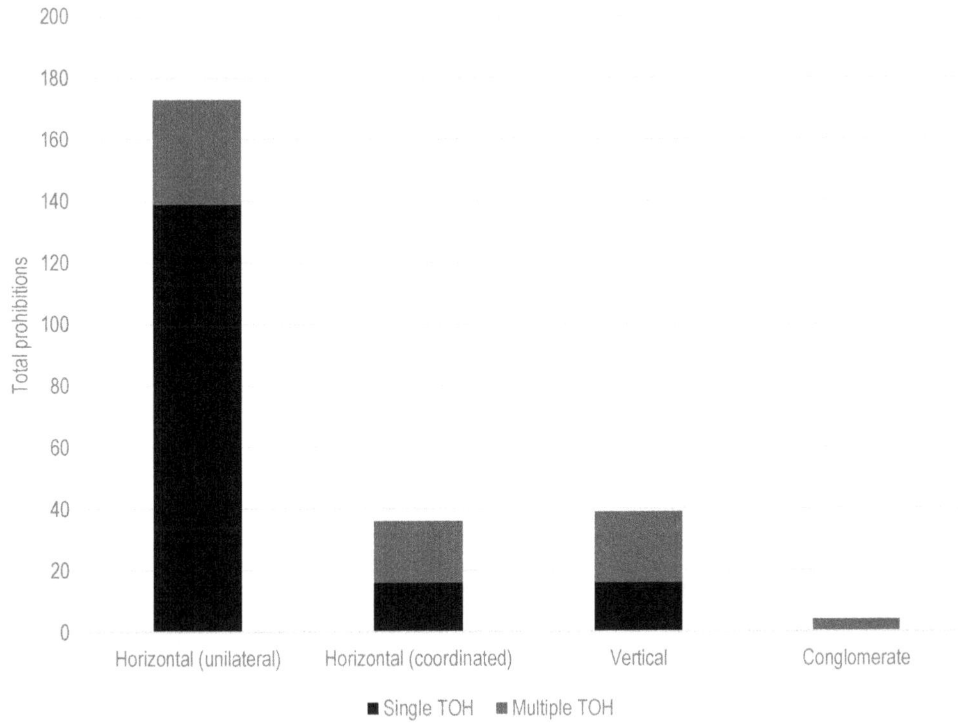

Note: Some prohibition decisions can rely on multiple theories of harm. This is indicated in the graph. Therefore, there are more theories of harm indicated in this figure than the number of prohibition decisions. There are also some jurisdictions that have other theories of harm, such as public interest theories of harm in South Africa, however these are not included in this figure.
Source: OECD with information from competition authorities' websites and annual reports shared by the authorities with the OECD.

StatLink https://stat.link/c9hd3p

The proportion of merger prohibition decisions between the various theories of harm has been relatively consistent over time, despite some variation. For example, 2019 had a peak of prohibition decisions considering vertical and conglomerate theories of harm.

Figure 3.9. Total prohibitions, by theory of harm and year, 2015-2022

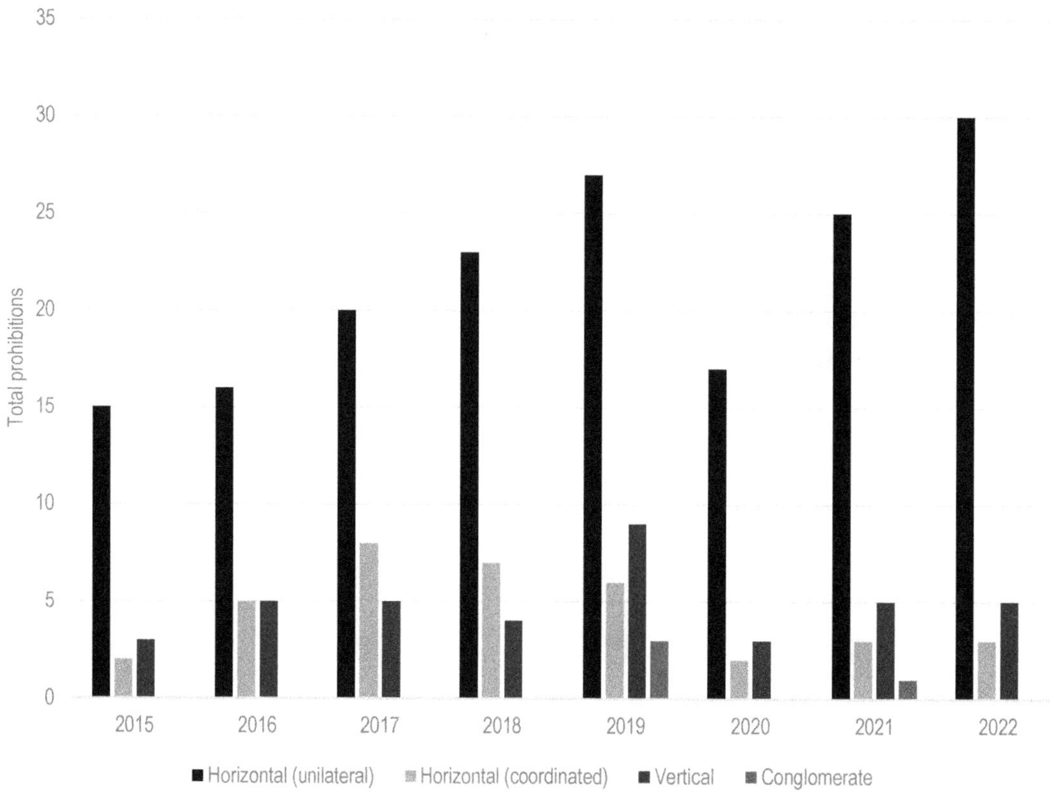

Note: Some prohibition decisions can rely on multiple theories of harm. This is indicated in the graph. Therefore, the number of times a theory of harm occurred exceeds the number of prohibition decisions. Moreover, although some jurisdictions have other (less common) theories of harm, such as public interest theories of harm in South Africa, they are not included in this figure.
Source: OECD with information from competition authorities' websites and annual reports shared by the authorities with the OECD.

StatLink https://stat.link/hwgeyd

Manufacturing and Retail Trade are industries with the most prohibitions

Prohibitions are more common in industries that are typically characterised by homogenous products and where there may be more likely issues related to a horizontal overlap, such as manufacturing and retail trade. However, there are also several prohibitions in the industry "information", which could relate, although imperfectly, to transactions in the digital markets.

Figure 3.10. Total prohibitions, by industry (NAICS), 2015-2022

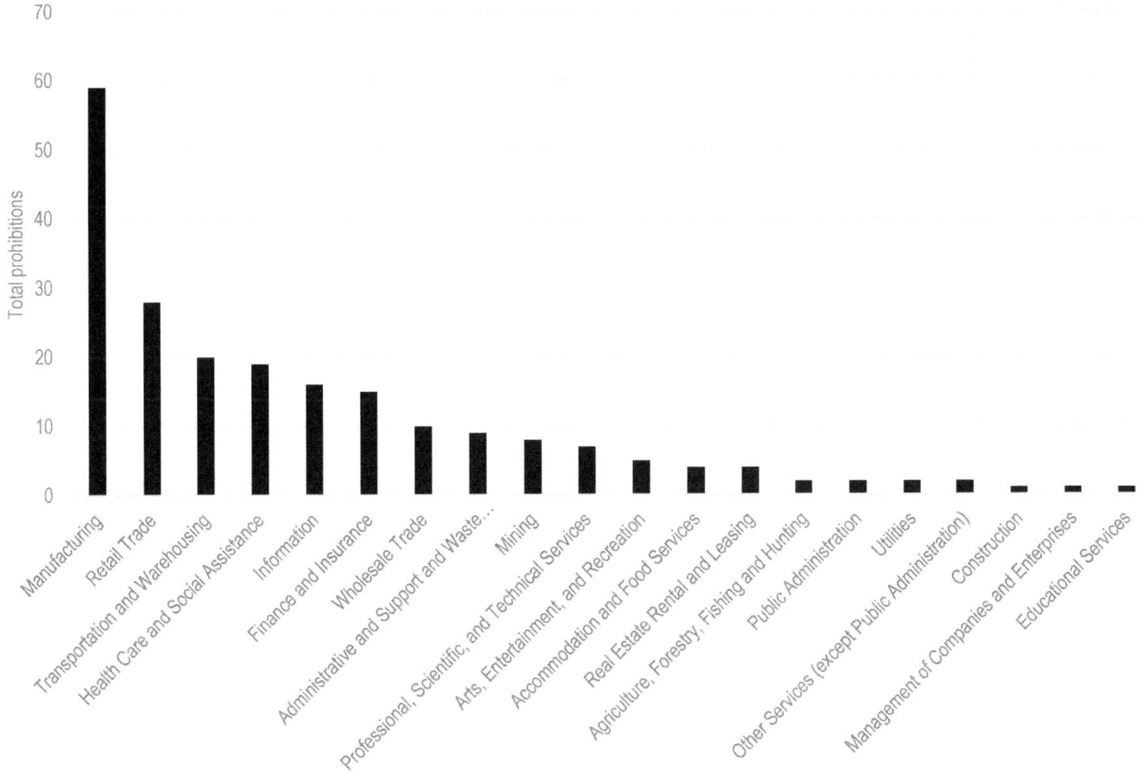

Source: OECD with information from competition authorities' websites and annual reports shared by the authorities with the OECD.

StatLink https://stat.link/uwv59y

Figure 3.11. Total prohibitions, by industry (NAICS) and TOH, 2015-2022

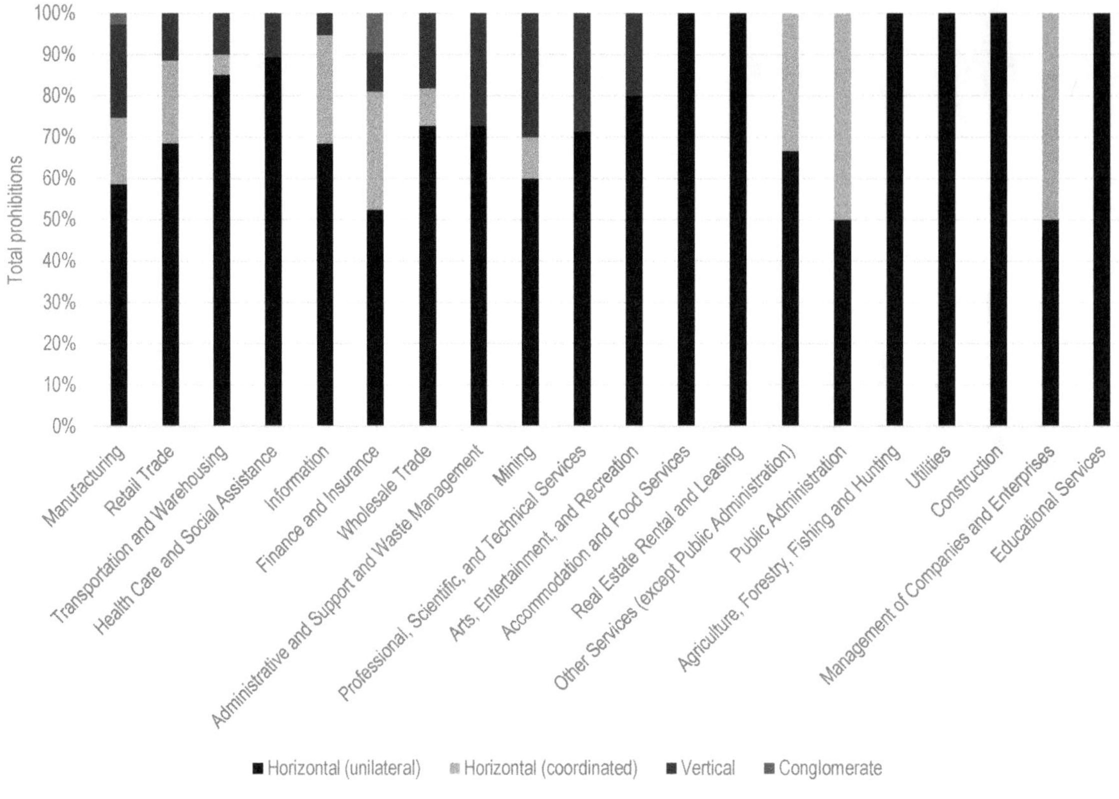

Source: OECD with information from competition authorities' websites and annual reports shared by the authorities with the OECD.

StatLink https://stat.link/apur7s

Annex A. Sources of CompStats

In 2018, under the guidance of the Bureau of the Competition Committee, the OECD Secretariat launched an initiative to develop a database of general statistics relating to competition agencies, including data on enforcement and information on advocacy initiatives.

Some statistics related to competition authorities' activities are already publicly available. However, this information is often dispersed, lacks consistency across time and jurisdictions, and is currently not used systematically to identify overall trends from which to draw policy lessons. This initiative fills this gap.

The OECD Secretariat collects data annually from: (i) competition authorities in OECD jurisdictions; (ii) authorities in non-OECD jurisdictions that are Participants or Associates in the OECD Competition Committee; and (iii) agencies in jurisdictions that are neither OECD member nor a participant or associate in the OECD Competition Committee but have expressed an interest to join the database.

Jurisdictions

The OECD CompStats database currently covers data from competition agencies in 77 jurisdictions, of which 38 jurisdictions are OECD jurisdictions (including the European Commission).[3]

There are four geographic regions used in the analysis: Americas, Asia-Pacific, Europe, and Middle East and Africa (MEA). The 77 jurisdictions in the OECD CompStats database are allocated to these geographic regions as follows (jurisdictions with an asterisk (*) are considered as OECD members for the data analysis):

- Americas (18): Argentina, Barbados, Brazil, Canada*, Chile*, Colombia*, Costa Rica*, Dominican Republic, Ecuador, El Salvador, Mexico*, Nicaragua, Panama, Paraguay, Peru, Trinidad and Tobago, United States*, and Uruguay.
- Asia-Pacific (15): Australia*, Bangladesh, Brunei Darussalam, Hong Kong (China), India, Indonesia, Japan*, Kazakhstan, Korea*, Malaysia, New Zealand*, Philippines, Singapore, Chinese Taipei, and Viet Nam.
- Europe (34): Albania, Austria*, Belgium*, Bulgaria, Croatia, Czechia*, Denmark*, European Commission*, Estonia, Finland*, France*, Germany*, Greece*, Hungary*, Iceland*, Ireland*, Italy*, Latvia*, Lithuania*, Luxembourg*, Malta, Montenegro, Netherlands*, Norway*, Poland*, Portugal*, Romania, Slovak Republic*, Slovenia*, Spain*, Sweden*, Switzerland*, Ukraine, and the United Kingdom*.
- MEA (10): Botswana, COMESA, Egypt, Israel*, Kenya, Mauritius, Saudi Arabia, South Africa, Tunisia, and Türkiye*.

Period

The OECD CompStats database contains eight years of annual data for the period 2015 to 2022.

Data

The following areas are currently covered in OECD CompStats database. There are 34 variables in total.

1. General information

- Budget
- Number of staff
- Number of competition staff

2. Cartels and other anticompetitive agreements

- Number of decisions
- Number of decisions per industry
- Number of decisions related to bid-rigging
- Number of decisions on vertical agreements
- Number of cases with settlements or plea bargain
- Number of cases with negotiated/consensual procedure for settling cases
- Number of leniency applications
- Number of ex-officio investigations launched
- Number of cases that used a dawn raid
- Total amount of fines imposed
- Number of companies fined
- Number of cases with fines on individual
- Number of cases with imprisonment of individual

3. Abuse of dominance/unilateral conduct

- Number of decisions
- Number of decisions per industry
- Number of cases with settlements or plea bargain
- Number of cases with negotiated/consensual procedure for settling cases
- Number of investigations launched
- Number of cases that used a dawn raid
- Total amount of fines imposed
- Number of companies fined

4. Mergers and acquisitions

- Number of notifications
- Number of Phase One (or single phase) clearances
- Number of Phase One (or single phase) clearances with remedies
- Number of Phase Two clearances (after an in-depth investigation)
- Number of Phase Two clearances with remedies
- Number of Phase Two prohibitions (or trials)

- Number of withdrawn notifications by merging parties in Phase Two

5. Advocacy

- Number of market studies
- Number of formal advocacy opinions issued to governments, regulators, legislators
- Number of advocacy events organised

6. Additional public data

In order to enrich the database and allow for better and in-depth analysis, the Secretariat has added the following variables to the database:

- Gross domestic product (GDP, current prices, purchasing power parity) and inflation data from the World Bank development indicators database. For some jurisdictions (Japan and Chinese Taipei), GDP data is from the International Monetary Fund (GDP, current prices, purchasing power parity).
- Population data from the United Nations World Population Prospects 2019
- Year of implementation of competition law
- Year of establishment of competition agency
- Year of adoption of merger control
- Characteristics of merger control regimes in CompStats (mandatory vs. voluntary merger notification, filing-fee requirements, selected criteria for establishing merger-notification threshold, use of simplified merger regime, and one-phase vs. two-phase approaches)

Competition Authorities in the OECD CompStats Database

The following competition authorities contributed with the information for the OECD CompStats Database.

Table A A.1. Competition Authorities in the OECD CompStats Database

Jurisdiction	Competition authority (name in English)
Albania	Competition Authority of Albania
Argentina	National Antitrust Commission
Australia	Australian Competition and Consumer Commission
Austria	The Federal Competition Authority
Bangladesh	Bangladesh Competition Commission
Barbados	The Barbados Fair Trading Commission
Belgium	Belgian Competition Authority
Botswana	Competition and Consumer Authority
Brazil	Administrative Council for Economic Defence
Brunei Darussalam	Competition Commission Brunei Darussalam Department of Competition and Consumer Affairs (DCCA) – Department of Economic Planning and Statistics – Ministry of Finance and Economy
Bulgaria	Commission on Protection of Competition
Canada	The Competition Bureau Canada
Chile	National Economic Prosecutor Tribunal for the Defense of Free Competition
Colombia	Superintendence of Industry and Commerce
COMESA	COMESA Competition Commission
Costa Rica	Commission for the Promotion of Competition Costa Rica Telecommunications Superintendency

Jurisdiction	Competition authority (name in English)
Croatia	Croatian Competition Agency
Czechia	Office for the Protection of Competition
Denmark	Danish Competition and Consumer Authority
Dominican Republic	National Commission for the Defence of Competition of the Dominican Republic
Ecuador	Superintendency for Control of Market Power
Egypt	Egyptian Competition Authority
El Salvador	Superintendency of Competition
Estonia	The Estonian Competition Authority
European Commission	European Commission Directorate-General for Competition
Finland	Finnish Competition and Consumer Authority
France	French Competition Authority
Germany	Federal Cartel Office
Greece	Hellenic Competition Commission
Hong Kong, China	Competition Commission (Hong Kong)
Hungary	Hungarian Competition Authority
Iceland	Icelandic Competition Authority
India	the Competition Commission of India
Indonesia	Indonesia Competition Commission
Ireland	Competition and Consumer Protection Commission
Israel	Israel Competition Authority
Italy	Italian Competition Authority
Japan	Japan Fair Trade Commission
Kazakhstan	Agency for the Protection and Development of Competition
Kenya	Competition Authority of Kenya
Korea	Korea Fair Trade Commission
Latvia	Competition Council of the Republic of Latvia
Lithuania	Competition Council of the Republic of Lithuania
Luxembourg	Competition Council
Malaysia	Malaysia Competition Commission
Malta	Malta Competition and Consumer Affairs Authority – The Office for Competition
Mauritius	Competition Commission of Mauritius
Mexico	Federal Economic Competition Commission Federal Institute of Telecommunications
Montenegro	Agency for Protection of Competition
Netherlands	Authority for Consumers and Markets
New Zealand	New Zealand Commerce Commission
Nicaragua	National Institute for the Promotion of Competition
Norway	Norwegian Competition Authority
Panama	Authority for Consumer Protection and Competition Defense
Paraguay	National Competition Commission
Peru	National Institute for the Defence of Free Competition and the Protection of Intellectual Property
Philippines	Philippine Competition Commission
Poland	Office of Competition and Consumer Protection
Portugal	Portuguese Competition Authority
Romania	Romanian Competition Council
Saudi Arabia	General Authority for Competition
Singapore	Competition and Consumer Commission of Singapore
Slovak Republic	Antimonopoly Office of the Slovak Republic
Slovenia	Slovenian Competition Protection Agency
South Africa	Competition Commission of South Africa
Spain	The Spanish National Commission of Markets and Competition
Sweden	Swedish Competition Authority
Switzerland	The Competition Commission

Jurisdiction	Competition authority (name in English)
Chinese Taipei	The Fair Trade Commission of Chinese Taipei
Trinidad and Tobago	Trinidad and Tobago Fair Trading Commission
Tunisia	Competition Council of Tunisia
Türkiye	Turkish Competition Authority
Ukraine	Antimonopoly Committee of Ukraine
United Kingdom	Competition and Markets Authority
United States	Department of Justice Antitrust Division Federal Trade Commission Bureau of Competition
Uruguay	Commission for the Promotion and Defense of Competition
Viet Nam	Vietnam Competition and Consumer Authority

Notes

[1] Budgets in real terms are calculated adjusting the values of nominal budgets by the inflation rate presented in each jurisdiction each year.

[2] It needs to be noted that the UK and New Zealand have voluntary merger regimes, which implies that those mergers that are notified are already more likely to be problematic. This is likely to affect the percentage of notified mergers that is challenged by the competition authority.

[3]The European Commission takes part in the work of the OECD, in accordance with the Supplementary Protocol to the Convention on the Organisation for Economic Co-operation and Development.

www.ingramcontent.com/pod-product-compliance
Lightning Source LLC
Chambersburg PA
CBHW061225240926
51846CB00006B/1363
* 9 7 8 9 2 6 4 4 6 6 3 7 1 *